jill dupleix

good cooking
the new essentials

photography by Peter Cassidy

Quadrille   Hardie Grant Books

Publishing director
Jane O'Shea
Creative director
Mary Evans
Project editor
Janet Illsley
Photographer
Peter Cassidy
Food stylist
Sunil Vijayakar
Props stylist
Roisin Nield
Production
Rebecca Short

NOTES
All spoon measures
are level;
1 tsp = 5 ml spoon;
1 tbsp = 15 ml spoon.

All eggs are free-range
and medium; all herbs
are fresh; all salt is
sea salt, and all pepper
is freshly ground black
pepper unless
otherwise stated.

Published in Australia in 2005
by Hardie Grant Books
85 High Street
Prahran, Victoria 3181
www.hardiegrant.com.au

Published in the UK in 2005
by Quadrille Publishing Limited
Alhambra House
27–31 Charing Cross Road
London WC2H 0LS

National Library of Australia
Cataloguing-in-Publication Data:
A catalogue record for this book is
available from the National Library
of Australia.

ISBN 1 74066 303 9

Printed and bound in China

10 9 8 7 6 5 4 3 2 1

Good cooking is all about making yourself feel good, in the kitchen and at the table. Sure, it's about generosity, hospitality and the inner glow that comes from feeding friends and family, but let's face it, if you're happy, they're happy. So work out how to use food to make yourself happy.

For me, that means re-writing the rulebook according to strictly modern principles, finding new and better ways with favourite flavours and much-loved classics. I love food, but only when it makes me feel good, not guilty. I love cooking, too, but not when I could be eating and drinking.

The new basics are fresher, lighter and simpler than the old basics, without the floury sauces, the cream, the pastry, and the deep-frying. Good cooking simply doesn't need them. All it needs is clever staples such as extra virgin olive oil, parmesan cheese, chillies, maple syrup, mustard, sea salt, herbs and chocolate, and additives – real ones – in the form of ginger, yoghurt, fresh lime, anchovies, sesame seeds and soy sauce. And lots of good ideas that can be used time and again.

Good shopping is 70% of good cooking. Buy great bacon and it won't ooze water in the pan. Buy real sourdough bread and it will be sturdy enough to take whatever you put on it. Buy fresh vegetables in season – preferably from a market stall – and you can cook them in the simplest way possible.

I am also a great believer in fast cooking, because speed captures the goodness in food. Every dish has its prime moment when flavour, colour and nutritional value are at their peak, and the recipes in this book try to capture that moment. Sometimes, though, slow, easy cooking is the answer, if only because the food does all the work and not you. I like that in a recipe.

Good cooking is its own reward. If we shop well and cook well, we eat well and feel well. Spread the joy.

soups

snacks

grilled tomato soup

A brilliant soup with a lovely smoky flavour from the grill. Serve as a summery first course, or as a meal with country bread.

SERVES 4

12 vine-ripened tomatoes
2 tbsp olive oil
2 garlic cloves, smashed
750 ml vegetable or chicken
  stock
250 ml tomato juice or V8
pinch of dried chilli flakes
pinch of sugar
sea salt and pepper
2 tbsp freshly grated parmesan
1 tbsp oregano leaves
1 tbsp extra virgin olive oil

Heat the grill. Brush the tomatoes with a little of the olive oil. Place under the grill for 15 to 20 minutes until the skin scorches and starts to peel. Leave to cool slightly.

Reserve 4 tomatoes for serving. Peel and roughly chop the rest, saving the juices. Combine the chopped flesh and juices in a saucepan with the remaining olive oil and the garlic, vegetable stock, tomato juice, chilli flakes, sugar, sea salt and pepper. Simmer for 15 minutes.

Taste for salt, pepper and sweetness, and adjust if necessary. Take out the garlic, if you remember.

Place the reserved tomatoes in four warm bowls and ladle the soup over the top. Scatter with the parmesan and oregano leaves, drizzle with the extra virgin olive oil and serve.

cocktail nachos

Who would think that lurking in a bag of tortilla chips are dozens of cute little canapés? If you can't get pickled jalapeños, use any mild, fresh green chilli.

MAKES 40

200 g cheddar cheese
100 g pickled green jalapeño chillies
40 salted corn tortilla chips
coriander leaves for serving

CHILLI SALSA

1 tbsp olive oil
3 shallots, peeled and finely diced
2 garlic cloves, crushed
200 g canned chopped tomatoes
2 tbsp chopped coriander
$1/2$ tsp dried chilli flakes
1 tsp sugar
$1/2$ tsp sea salt
squeeze of lime juice

To make the chilli salsa, heat the olive oil in a pan and cook the shallots until soft. Add the garlic, tomatoes, coriander, chilli, sugar and salt, and cook down for 20 minutes until thick and sludgy. Add the lime juice and whiz to a smooth sauce using a blender, then cool.

Heat the oven to 200°C/Gas 6. Coarsely grate the cheese and finely slice the jalapeño chillies. Lay out 40 unbroken corn chips on two baking trays, and top each one with a little grated cheese and a slice or two of jalapeño.

Bake for 5 to 10 minutes or until the cheese melts and the corn chips are hot and crisp.

Add a tiny dab of chilli salsa and a coriander leaf to each corn chip, and serve hot.

mussels in tomato broth

This is one of those dishes that is an open invitation to slurp, as you dig out mussels and soak up the soupy juices with crackers or crusty bread. If you want a more polite chowder, then remove the mussels from their shells.

SERVES 4

500 g floury potatoes
1 onion, peeled
1 tbsp butter
4 bacon rashers, diced
3 celery stalks, finely diced
1 tsp thyme leaves
3 tbsp chopped parsley, plus
   extra for serving
400 g can chopped tomatoes
sea salt and pepper
1.5 kg mussels, rinsed
125 ml white wine

Peel and dice the potatoes. Halve and finely slice the onion. Melt the butter in a large frying pan and cook the bacon, onion and celery for 10 minutes. Add the potatoes, thyme, parsley, tomatoes, seasoning and 1 litre water, stirring well. Bring to the boil and simmer for 20 minutes.

Scrub the mussels, discarding any that are broken, and yank out the little beards. Bring the white wine and 200 ml water to the boil in a large pan. Add the mussels, cover tightly and cook for 2 minutes, then use a slotted spoon to remove them as soon as they open, discarding any unopened shells.

Strain the mussel broth through a muslin-lined sieve into the soup. Add the mussels to the broth, shelled or unshelled, along with any juices. Gently heat for 5 minutes.

Serve in warm soup bowls, scattered with a little extra chopped parsley. Serve with crackers, for crumbling into the soup as you eat.

sherry clams with jamon

Cured ham and sherry give this clam broth a wonderfully rounded Spanish flavour. Serve as part of a meal of tapas, with a glass of lightly chilled, fine Jerez (sherry).

SERVES 4

500 g small, fresh clams
50 g cured ham or jamon,
 thickly sliced
1 small onion, peeled
2 tbsp olive oil
50 ml Spanish sherry
1 tbsp chopped flat-leaf
 parsley

Soak the clams in a bowl of cold water for 1 hour, then drain well. Cut the ham into 1 cm squares.

Finely slice the onion. Heat the olive oil in a heavy frying pan and cook the onion for 5 minutes until soft. Add the ham and stir it through. Add the sherry and bring to the boil.

Add the clams and clamp the lid on tightly. Allow to boil for 2 minutes, then give the pan a big shake. Remove the lid and use a pair of tongs to remove the clams as they open.

When all the clams have opened (throw out any that don't), return them to the pan and toss well in the sauce. Scatter with the chopped parsley and serve warm or at room temperature.

extra

pinchos & montaditos
Turn a simple dish into a casual, easy meal of Spanish tapas by adding a few little snackettes, defined as good-things-on-bread that you eat with your fingers.

to make pinchos slice a crusty baguette on the diagonal, and lightly grill. Top with folds of roasted sweet red pepper and sliced jamon (cured ham); smoky piquillo peppers with olives and anchovies; manchego cheese and membrillo quince paste; sizzled chorizo sausage and white bean purée; seared prawns with aïoli; smoked salmon and piquillo peppers; sliced tomatoes and anchovies.

serve with lots of chilled sherry or cold beers.

rocket cocktail

This is an amazing way to crank-start the appetite – dramatic and elegant, with a chlorophyllic, peppery, lemony flavour that is missing from your normal everyday cocktails. I discovered it at Heinz Beck's food-forward La Pergola restaurant at the Rome Cavalieri Hilton, and fell instantly in love with it.

SERVES 6

100 g rocket leaves
500 ml ginger ale
250 g lemon sorbet

In a blender, whiz the rocket, ginger ale and lemon sorbet at high speed until you have a smooth green liquid. Pour into chilled 100ml martini glasses and serve.

You can make the cocktail beforehand, but it should always be icy cold, and should always be re-blended for a few seconds before serving. Think of it as a chilled rocket gazpacho, and slip in a dash of frozen vodka if you like.

chive brot

I came across this wild-tasting, chive-carpeted rye bread in Vienna, and again in Munich, and co-opted it for my favourite *smorrebrod* meal of salmon, boiled egg and salmon roe. To serve with drinks, make it in miniature with quail eggs.

SERVES 4

1 medium egg
50 g chives, plus extra for
   serving
4 thin, square slices
   pumpernickel or rye bread
50 g cream cheese or unsalted
   butter
400 g smoked or cured
   salmon, finely sliced
50 g salmon roe
freshly ground black pepper
1 lemon, quartered

Add the egg to a small pan of hot water and bring to the boil. Simmer for 8 minutes, then drain and cool under cold running water.

With a pair of scissors, finely snip the chives (and I mean *finely* snip) and arrange on a flat plate.

Spread the rye bread with the cream cheese or butter, right to the edges. Lay the bread spread-side down on the chives, pressing lightly, to cover each slice with a fine layer of chives, from edge to edge.

Peel and finely slice the egg, using an egg-slicer. Lay the chive bread on a plate, top with a fold of salmon, an egg slice and a teaspoonful of salmon roe, and grind over some black pepper. Add a whole chive and serve with a wedge of lemon.

miang kum

These little Thai leaf-wrapped appetisers pack a mean punch of hot, sour, sweet and smoky flavours. Cha plu leaves are available from Thai specialists. Swap the salmon for shredded, cooked chicken, pork or shrimps if you like.

MAKES 12

12 cha plu, spinach or
   lettuce leaves
200 g hot-smoked salmon fillet
2 kaffir lime leaves
1 tbsp finely diced lime
2 tbsp peanuts, chopped
1 tbsp chopped coriander
50 g salmon roe

HOT-SOUR-SWEET SAUCE

2 shallots, finely sliced
1 garlic clove, crushed
$^{1}/_{2}$ small red chilli, diced
2 tbsp peanuts
100 g soft brown sugar
1 tbsp fish sauce
1 tbsp tamarind concentrate

To make the sauce, pound the shallots in a mortar with the garlic, chilli and peanuts to a paste. In a saucepan, mix this paste with the sugar, fish sauce, tamarind and 1 tbsp water, and bring to the boil, stirring. Simmer for 5 minutes, stirring, until thick and syrupy. Cool.

Wash and dry the leaves and set out on a tray. Shred the smoked salmon into bite-sized pieces, discarding any bones and skin.

Fold each kaffir lime leaf in half along the spine, then cut away and discard the spine. Cut the leaves lengthways into extremely thin strips and set aside.

Top each whole leaf with some smoked salmon and a teaspoonful of sauce. (If the sauce is too firm, beat in a spoonful of boiling water.) Scatter with diced lime, peanuts and coriander. Top with a little salmon roe, scatter with shredded kaffir lime leaf, wrap and eat.

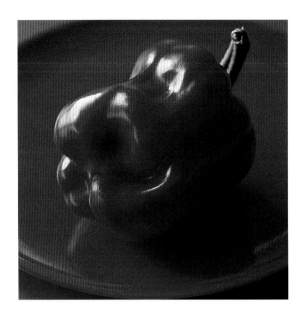

red pepper hot cakes

I grew up on fritters made with leftover roast lamb, and have loved the genre ever since. Make these with cooked chicken, duck or pork instead of ham, or with leftover potatoes and peas.

SERVES 4

1 large sweet red pepper
1 thick slice ham, diced
2 tbsp freshly grated parmesan
2 tbsp chopped parsley
sea salt and pepper
1 tbsp vegetable oil
BATTER
100 g plain flour
1 tsp baking powder
good pinch of cayenne pepper
2 eggs, separated
150 ml milk

To make the batter, sift the flour, baking powder and cayenne into a bowl. Add the egg yolks and lightly mix, then slowly add the milk, beating with a wooden spoon until smooth. Beat the egg whites in another bowl until peaky, and fold into the batter.

Finely dice the pepper, discarding the core and seeds. Add to the batter with the ham, parmesan, parsley, sea salt and pepper, mixing lightly.

Heat half the oil in a non-stick frying pan. When hot, drop 4 tablespoons of the batter into the pan, keeping them separate. Turn the heat to low. When holes appear on top of the batter, turn and cook the other side for 3 to 4 minutes until golden. Remove and keep warm.

Heat the remaining oil in the pan and make another 4 fritters. Serve for brunch, lunch or supper, with an avocado salad.

sweet potato & bean soup

This simple soup would be quite nice on its own – but add a little curry powder and your spoon just can't leave it alone. Serve it in small bowls as a first course, or with warm Indian bread for a family supper.

SERVES 4

1 kg orange-fleshed sweet potatoes
1.2 litres boiling water or vegetable stock
sea salt and pepper
400 g can white beans (eg haricot or cannellini), drained and rinsed
1 tsp good curry powder, or more
80 g low-fat yoghurt
pinch of paprika
2 tbsp coriander or parsley leaves

Peel the sweet potatoes, cut into small cubes and put into a pan. Add the boiling water or stock, sea salt and pepper, and bring to the boil. Simmer for 15 minutes or until the sweet potato is soft.

Add half the beans and the curry powder, stirring well, then whiz in a food processor in batches, being careful not to overfill the bowl.

Return to the pan, add the remaining whole beans and heat gently. If too thick, add extra boiling water. Taste for salt, pepper and curry powder.

Ladle the soup into warm bowls. Swirl a generous dollop of yoghurt into each bowl and sprinkle with a little paprika. Scatter with coriander or parsley and serve.

veg salads

summer vegetable carpaccio

The new carpaccio is of vegetables, not beef – finely sliced, crisp summer vegetables dressed with a lemony vinaigrette. If you grow small, tender carrots or green beans, or have edible flowers, such as chive flowers, add them too.

SERVES 4

2 celery stalks
8 small pink radishes
10 broad bean pods
small wedge of parmesan for shaving
1 fennel bulb
1 tbsp salted capers, rinsed

DRESSING
2 tbsp extra virgin olive oil
1 tbsp lemon juice
sea salt and pepper

Finely slice the celery on an extreme diagonal. Finely slice the radishes. Pod the broad beans, and cook in simmering water for 5 minutes or until tender. Cool under running water, and peel off the outer skins.

Using a vegetable peeler, carefully shave thin slices of parmesan onto a sheet of paper or foil. To make the dressing, whisk the olive oil, lemon juice and seasoning together in a bowl.

At the last minute, trim off the stalks and any tough outer leaves from the fennel, then slice across the bulb as finely as possible. Drop the sliced fennel into the dressing and toss well.

Scatter the fennel lightly over four dinner plates. Toss the celery, radishes and broad beans in the remaining dressing and scatter on top, as if you are topping a pizza. Drizzle with any remaining dressing, and finish with the capers and parmesan shavings.

avocado & grapefruit salad

Rich creamy avocado is cut back by the citrus sharpness of grapefruit in this Israeli-inspired salad. It's brilliant for a brunchy breakfast, and teams well with grilled salmon, tuna or mackerel for dinner.

SERVES 4

1 ripe grapefruit
2 tbsp extra virgin olive oil
  or walnut oil
sea salt and pepper
2 large ripe avocadoes
2 little gem or baby cos
  lettuces
3 tbsp coriander leaves,
  roughly chopped
pinch of pink peppercorns,
  crushed

Hold the grapefruit over a bowl to catch the juices, and peel it thickly, removing all white pith. Cut the grapefruit between the membrane into segments. Whisk the juices with the olive or walnut oil, sea salt and pepper to make the dressing.

Cut each avocado in half lengthways, remove the stone and peel off the skin. Cut the flesh into long, thin slices and carefully toss in the dressing with the grapefruit.

Separate the lettuce leaves, wash and pat dry, then tear into bite-sized pieces. Lightly toss the avocado and grapefruit with the leaves and half the coriander, then drain off any excess dressing.

Serve in cute cocktail glasses or on a large platter. Scatter with crushed pink peppercorns and the remaining coriander.

asian herb salad

This has a wonderfully wild freshness about it, which is achieved by massive overuse of delicate herbs and my all-time favourite sweet-and-sour vinaigrette.

SERVES 4

100 g rocket leaves
100 g mint
100 g basil
100 g coriander
25 g chervil
100 g canned bamboo shoots

DRESSING

2 shallots, peeled, halved
  and finely sliced
1 tbsp rice vinegar
1 tsp caster sugar
2 tbsp extra virgin olive oil
1 tsp sesame oil
1 tbsp mirin
sea salt and pepper

For the dressing, mix the shallots, rice vinegar and sugar together in a small bowl and set aside.

Trim any excess stalks from the rocket and pick the herb leaves from their stalks. Rinse and spin dry the rocket and herbs. Cut the bamboo shoots into matchsticks.

To make the dressing, whisk the olive oil, sesame oil, mirin, sea salt and pepper together in a large bowl. Stir in the shallot mixture, then taste and adjust the flavours.

Very lightly toss the rocket, bamboo shoots and the herbs in the dressing and serve, with chopsticks.

rumbledethumps

It's cold. You're feeling blue. You need rumbledethumps, an irresistibly comforting dish from the Scottish Borders in which potatoes are mashed with cabbage and topped with melting cheese. If you're feeling really depressed, top with a fried egg.

SERVES 4

500 g all-purpose potatoes
400 g savoy cabbage
sea salt and pepper
6 spring onions, finely
  chopped
2 tbsp butter
30 g cheddar, freshly grated
30 g parmesan, freshly grated

Heat the oven to 180°C/Gas 4. Peel the potatoes and cut into rough chunks. Remove any tough outer leaves from the cabbage and finely slice the leaves.

Cook the potatoes in a large pan of simmering, salted water for 10 minutes, then add the cabbage and cook for a further 10 minutes or until both are tender, but not overly soft. Add the spring onions for the last minute of cooking, then drain well.

Add the butter and most of the cheese, and mash together well, seasoning with salt and pepper.

You can serve the rumbledethumps at this stage, or dump it into a buttered ovenproof dish, scatter with the remaining grated cheese and bake for 20 to 30 minutes until lightly browned and steaming hot.

fruit & vegetable tagine

This rich, fruity, spicy, aromatic tagine brings vegetables to life. Serve with steamy golden couscous, Morocco's national dish.

SERVES 4

1 large onion, peeled
2 tbsp olive oil
2 garlic cloves, crushed
1 tsp ground coriander
1/2 tsp ground ginger
1/2 tsp saffron powder
400 g sweet potato, peeled
8 baby carrots, peeled
400 g can chopped tomatoes
400 ml vegetable stock
8 green olives, cracked
8 dried apricots or figs
1 tsp harissa or chilli sauce
1 tbsp runny honey
2 cinnamon sticks
400 g courgettes (zucchini)
8 plump medjool dates

Halve and finely slice the onion. Heat the olive oil in a heavy pan and gently cook the onion for 10 minutes, stirring well. Add the garlic, coriander, ginger and saffron, stirring well.

Roughly chop the sweet potato and add to the pan with the carrots, tomatoes, stock, olives, apricots or figs, harissa or chilli sauce, honey, sea salt, pepper and cinnamon sticks, stirring. Cover the pan and simmer for 15 minutes.

Roughly chop the courgettes and add to the pan with the dates. Simmer for a further 15 minutes or until the vegetables are tender but not falling apart. Taste for salt and pepper and serve hot, with couscous.

extra

easy couscous Combine 300 g 'instant' couscous, 2 tbsp extra virgin olive oil, salt and pepper in a bowl. Add 500 ml boiling water, cover and leave for 10 minutes. Fluff up with a fork. Keep warm over a pan of simmering water until ready to serve.

green couscous Add 2 tbsp each lemon juice, finely chopped coriander and chopped parsley with the water.

red couscous Add 400 g can tomatoes, drained and chopped, 2 cinnamon sticks and 1 tsp ground cumin with the water.

lemon couscous Add 2 tbsp diced preserved lemon, 1 tsp dried mint, 2 tbsp finely chopped mint and 1 tbsp toasted flaked almonds with the water.

moroccan café salad

A hearty, warm salad of roasted vegetables, tossed with a fruity, saffron dressing and served with feathery leaves of frisée and the crunch of pine nuts.

SERVES 4

2 courgettes (zucchini)
2 aubergines (eggplants)
2 parsnips, peeled
2 tbsp olive oil
1 tbsp thyme sprigs
sea salt and pepper
200 g cherry tomatoes
1 frisée (curly endive)
1 tbsp pine nuts, toasted

DRESSING

good pinch of saffron threads
  (about 20)
1 tbsp raisins or sultanas
2 tbsp extra virgin olive oil
1 tbsp red wine vinegar
1 tsp Dijon mustard

Heat the oven to 200°C/Gas 6. For the dressing, soak the saffron and raisins or sultanas in 2 tbsp boiling water and set aside.

Trim the courgettes, aubergines and parsnips and quarter lengthways. Toss in the olive oil with the thyme, sea salt and pepper, then tip into a roasting pan. Roast for 30 minutes.

Toss the vegetables, add the cherry tomatoes and roast for a further 10 minutes or until the vegetables are scorched and soft. Allow to cool for 10 minutes.

To make the dressing, whisk the olive oil, wine vinegar, mustard, sea salt and pepper in a large bowl with the saffron, raisins and soaking water.

Trim the frisée and tear the leaves in half. Toss the leaves in half the dressing and arrange in serving bowls. Toss the warm vegetables and cherry tomatoes in the remaining dressing and strew over the top. Scatter with toasted pine nuts and serve.

soy sauce

Soy sauce adds instant complexity with its mysterious fermented soy bean flavour. Keep a bottle handy, and don't just use it for the stir-fry. Add a dash of soy to soups, stews and roasts for another layer of flavour.

which soy? Dark soy is black and strong, light soy is dark brown and salty, tamari is wheat-free, and Japanese soy is light, elegant and all-purpose (eg Kikkoman, Yamasa).

spice up your soy Add 4 star anise, 3 dried chillies and 20 peppercorns to 300 ml soy sauce. Leave for a week in a screw-top jar, and use for marinades, dips and noodles.

lemon soy dip Mix 3 tbsp soy sauce with 1 tbsp lemon juice. Cut sashimi-quality tuna into bite-sized cubes and dip into the lemon-soy. Serve with wasabi paste.

sweet soy omelette Beat 2 eggs with 1 tsp soy, 1 tsp mirin, sea salt and pepper. Heat 1 tsp oil in a wok, swirling to coat the entire surface. Add the egg and swirl again. Cook briefly until set, loosen the edges and turn out. Roll and finely slice to add to stir-fries, noodles and rice.

honey roast carrots Scrub and trim two bunches of baby carrots. Coat them in 2 tbsp soy, 2 tbsp olive oil, 1 tsp honey, sea salt and pepper. Roast at 200°C/Gas 6 for 20 minutes or until browned and tender.

steamed soy fish Mix 2 tbsp soy with 1 tsp sesame oil and 1 tbsp Chinese rice wine. Pour over two 180 g white fish fillets on a heatproof platter. Scatter with shredded ginger, chilli and coriander and steam for 10 minutes or until cooked. Serve with rice or noodles.

double happiness beans

Salted black beans are preserved, fermented soy beans, available from Chinese food stores. I made up the bit about double happiness, but the combination of the two beans certainly does it for me.

SERVES 4

2 tbsp salted black beans

2 cm knob of ginger, peeled

300 g fine green beans

1 sweet red pepper

sea salt

2 tbsp vegetable oil

1 garlic clove, smashed

$^1/_2$ small red chilli, finely sliced

1 tbsp Chinese rice wine or
   dry sherry

2 tbsp soy sauce

1 tsp sesame oil

1 tsp cornflour mixed with
   1 tbsp cold water

Soak the black beans in cold water for 10 minutes, then drain. Cut the ginger into thin matchsticks. Top, but don't tail the green beans. Cut the red pepper into thin strips, discarding the core and seeds.

Cook the green beans and red pepper in a pan of simmering, salted water for 3 minutes, then drain and refresh under cold running water. Drain again, and pat dry with a clean tea-towel.

Heat the oil in a wok or frying pan, then add the garlic, ginger and chilli, tossing well. Add the green beans and red pepper, and toss well for 2 minutes over a high heat. Add the black beans, rice wine, soy sauce and sesame oil and toss well for a further minute.

Add the cornflour mixture and toss over the heat until the sauce thickens and coats the vegetables. Serve hot, with steamed rice.

airport potatoes

I pinched this from the warming trays of the cafeteria at Rome Airport, long a source of wonderful ideas. I often serve it with grilled fish or chicken, but you could make a meal of it.

SERVES 4

1 kg all-purpose potatoes, peeled
1 tbsp olive oil for pan
sea salt and pepper
400 g can chopped tomatoes
2 tbsp extra virgin olive oil
2 garlic cloves, crushed
$1/2$ tsp dried oregano
1 tbsp salted capers, rinsed
2 tbsp roughly chopped parsley
200 g cherry tomatoes

Heat the oven to 190°C/Gas 5. Finely slice the potatoes and roughly layer over the base of an oiled roasting pan. Add 250 ml water, season with salt and pepper, then cover the pan with foil and bake for 30 minutes.

Combine the canned tomatoes with the extra virgin olive oil, garlic, oregano, capers, half the chopped parsley, and sea salt and pepper.

Remove the foil, and pour the tomato mixture over the potatoes. Cut the cherry tomatoes in half and scatter on top. Bake for a further 30 minutes until the potatoes are tender and starting to crisp at the edges. Scatter with the remaining chopped parsley and serve.

zucchini with mint & almonds

Courgettes or zucchini? This speedy dish has such an Italian accent, I had to call it zucchini. Besides, it really belongs to New York chef Jimmy Bradley of The Red Cat, who cuts the zucchini very, very finely and tosses them over a superhigh heat for just a few seconds.

SERVES 4

500 g courgettes (zucchini)
2 tbsp olive oil
25 g flaked almonds
1 tbsp mint leaves, torn if large
sea salt and pepper

Cut off the ends of the courgettes, then cut into three short sections. Slice each section lengthways, then cut each slice into matchsticks.

Heat the olive oil in a frying pan over medium heat, add the flaked almonds and toast until golden.

Add the courgettes to the hot pan, and toss over high heat for a minute or two until just cooked, but don't overcook until limp.

Scatter with mint leaves, sea salt and pepper, and serve on four warm plates as a first course, or one large platter as a side dish.

grains

greens

grains

greens

goat cheese, beans & walnuts

Compatible flavours are often natural companions. Whenever I eat this, I always imagine goats grazing contentedly under walnut trees, their milk transformed into fresh tangy cheese. This magical place may not actually exist, but it should.

SERVES 4

300 g fresh goat cheese
  (in log form)
600 g fine green beans
100 g walnut halves
sea salt and pepper
MARINADE
100 ml extra virgin olive oil
1 tbsp walnut oil
2 shallots, peeled and finely
  sliced
1 garlic clove, flattened
1 tsp thyme leaves
1 tsp coriander seeds, cracked
1 tsp fennel seeds

To marinate the goat cheese, cut it into thick slices and arrange in a single layer on a platter. Combine the olive and walnut oils, shallots, garlic, thyme, coriander and fennel seeds, then pour over the cheese. Cover with plastic film, and leave until serving.

Top, but don't tail the green beans. Cook in simmering, salted water for 5 minutes until tender, and drain. Toast the walnut halves in a hot dry pan until fragrant.

Heat the grill. Drain off a little marinade from the cheese and toss the beans in it, adding sea salt and pepper. Arrange the beans on large serving plates.

Gently lift the cheese slices onto a sheet of foil and put under the grill until just melted. Place on top of the beans, and spoon over the remaining marinade. Scatter with the toasted walnuts and serve.

abruzzese lentil soup

You could virtually live on this rustic, slow-cooked soup. Lentils are low in fat and high in protein, easy to cook and taste delicious. Look for the small lentils from Umbria or Abruzzo in Italy, or from Puy in France, which hold their shape well and taste deliciously nutty.

SERVES 6

250 g small brown or green
   lentils
2 garlic cloves, smashed
2 bay leaves
1 onion, peeled and halved
2 celery stalks
2 carrots, peeled
2 tbsp olive oil
400 g can chopped tomatoes
400 g can chickpeas, drained
sea salt and pepper
2 tbsp chopped parsley
freshly grated parmesan for
   serving

Rinse the lentils, and place in a pan with the garlic, bay leaves and 1.5 litres cold water. Cook for 30 minutes or until almost tender, skimming occasionally.

In the meantime, finely slice the onion and celery, and dice the carrots. Heat the olive oil in a large saucepan. Add the onion, carrots and celery, and cook, stirring often, for 10 minutes.

Add the tomatoes, stir well, then add the lentils and their cooking water. Simmer for 20 minutes until nice and soupy.

Add the chickpeas, sea salt and pepper, and simmer for a further 10 minutes or longer, adding extra water as necessary.

Stir in the chopped parsley and ladle into warm soup bowls. Serve with grated parmesan.

bulghur prawn salad

Juicy, crunchy, wheaty bulghur or burghul (that funny grainy stuff in tabbouleh) is the perfect foil for prawns, avocado and preserved lemon, in one of the freshest salads around. Drizzle with parsley oil for even more freshness and flavour.

SERVES 4

200 g fine bulghur wheat

12 raw prawns in shells

sea salt and pepper

3 tbsp extra virgin olive oil, plus extra for serving

2 tbsp lemon juice, plus extra for serving

1 avocado

2 tbsp roughly chopped coriander

2 tbsp chopped preserved lemon

Put the bulghur into a large heatproof bowl and pour on 400 ml boiling water. Stir and leave to stand for 30 minutes.

Cook the prawns lightly in a pan of simmering, salted water, until just pink and no longer transparent. Remove and allow to cool.

In a large bowl, whisk the olive oil and lemon juice with sea salt and pepper. Cut the avocado in half, remove the stone, peel and chop. Add the chopped avocado, coriander and preserved lemon to the dressing.

Drain the bulghur of any unabsorbed water, then squeeze dry and toss with the dressing.

Peel the prawns, leaving the tails. Toss in a little extra olive oil and lemon juice, and arrange on top of the bulghur salad.

extra

parsley or basil oil
Use to add brilliant colour, flavour and fragrance to salads, soups, fish and – best of all – roast chicken.

to prepare plunge 75 g flat-leaf parsley or basil into a pan of fast boiling water for 15 seconds. Remove and immediately plunge into a bowl of cold water filled with ice cubes. Drain and squeeze dry. Roughly chop and whiz with 75 ml olive oil for 10 seconds. Add 75 ml vegetable oil and whiz for 1 minute. Leave to strain through dampened muslin or a sieve lined with a paper coffee filter for several hours.

store in an airtight jar in the fridge and use within 1 week, or freeze in ice cube trays for future use.

summer rice with basil

Think of this as a hot rice salad, a summery pilaf that makes a wonderful change from the daily salad – especially if it involves everybody's favourite summer staples: tomato, basil and zucchini.

SERVES 4

3 shallots, peeled
1 celery stalk
1 tbsp butter
1 tbsp olive oil
300 g arborio rice
125 ml white wine
1.2 litres hot chicken or
    vegetable stock
2 large ripe red tomatoes
2 courgettes (zucchini)
1 tbsp extra virgin olive oil
sea salt and pepper
2 tbsp basil leaves
freshly grated parmesan for
    serving

Finely slice the shallots and celery. Melt the butter with the olive oil in a heavy pan and cook the shallots and celery, stirring, until softened. Add the rice and stir until well coated. Add the wine and allow to bubble for a minute or two, stirring, until absorbed.

Add all but one ladleful of stock, stir well, and bring to the boil. Reduce the heat to very low, cover tightly, and cook gently for 18 to 20 minutes, when the surface of the rice should be pock-marked with small holes.

Meanwhile, cut the tomatoes in half, squeeze out the seeds, then cut the flesh into small dice and set aside. Trim and dice the courgettes.

Add the remaining stock and the courgettes to the rice and cook, stirring, for 5 minutes.

Stir in the tomatoes, extra virgin olive oil, and sea salt and pepper to taste. Scatter with basil leaves and serve with grated parmesan.

greek bean stew with feta

The traditional beans to use are dried gigantes or lima (butter) beans, which need overnight soaking and long, slow cooking, but for this I-haven't-got-all-day version use canned cannellini, butter or red kidney beans instead.

SERVES 4

1 onion, peeled
2 tbsp olive oil, plus extra
   for serving
2 garlic cloves, crushed
400 g can chopped tomatoes
1 tbsp tomato purée (paste)
2 bay leaves
2 tbsp finely chopped parsley
2 tbsp finely chopped dill
1 tsp sea salt
$1/2$ tsp pepper
$1/2$ tsp paprika
1 tbsp sugar
600 g canned beans
100 g feta cheese

Halve and finely slice the onion. Heat the olive oil in a heavy pan and fry the onion until soft but not browned. Add the garlic, tomatoes, tomato purée and 500 ml water. Stir in the bay leaves, parsley, half the dill, sea salt, pepper, paprika and sugar, and bring to a simmer.

Simmer, partly covered, for 20 to 30 minutes until nice and thick. Drain and rinse the beans, add to the stew, and simmer gently for another 10 minutes.

Rinse the feta cheese, pat dry and cut into chunky cubes. Add to the pan and simmer for another 5 minutes until the cheese is soft.

Serve in small bowls, drizzled with a little extra olive oil and scattered with the remaining dill. Serve hot or at room temperature, with some warm flat bread and a Greek salad.

sausage & parsnip risotto

Risotto is one of my favourite cold-weather dishes, the culinary equivalent of a blazing fire and cashmere cushions.

SERVES 4

2 parsnips
sea salt and pepper
1 onion, peeled
2 tbsp butter
1 tbsp olive oil
2 Italian pork sausages
4 rosemary sprigs
350 g arborio rice
150 ml light red wine
1.2 litres hot chicken stock
1 tbsp tomato purée (paste)
1 tbsp finely chopped flat-leaf
   parsley
1 tbsp freshly grated parmesan

Peel the parsnips, slice thickly and cook in simmering, salted water for 10 minutes. Drain and set aside.

Halve and finely slice the onion. Melt half of the butter with the olive oil in a heavy pan, add the onion and cook for a few minutes until softened. Skin the sausages and pinch small portions into the pan. Fry until well browned, then take out half the sausage and set aside.

Add the rosemary and rice to the pan and stir until well coated. Add the wine and allow to bubble for 2 minutes, stirring, until absorbed.

Add a ladleful of stock to the rice, and stir until it is absorbed. Add another ladleful and stir constantly, but calmly, with a wooden spoon until absorbed. Continue this process for around 15 to 20 minutes until the rice is cooked and still creamy.

Add the tomato purée, sliced parsnips, reserved sausage, remaining butter, sea salt, pepper, parsley and parmesan. Heat through and serve.

sesame

Sesame seeds – black or white – add fresh nutty flavour to breads, cakes and salads. Then there is fragrant, toasty sesame oil and nutty, creamy sesame paste (tahini), a brilliant stand-by for instant dips and sauces.

toast sesame seeds in a hot, dry pan for a few seconds before using, for extra flavour.

honey sesame peaches Peel 4 fresh peaches – dip in boiling water for 5 seconds then peel off the skin. Cut in half and remove stones. Drizzle with a little honey, scatter with sesame seeds and place under a hot grill for 3 minutes until golden.

sesame asparagus Lightly toss cooked asparagus in 1 tsp sesame oil. Sprinkle with sesame seeds and serve.

sesame prawns Take 8 fresh prawns, remove heads and snip off legs. Cut in half lengthways, keeping the shell intact, then flatten. Brush prawns with sesame oil, scatter with salt and 1 tbsp sesame seeds, then scorch under a hot grill for 3 minutes.

dip into dukkah In a hot dry pan, toast 100 g white sesame seeds, 100 g blanched almonds, 50 g coriander seeds and 10 g cumin seeds until fragrant, stirring. Cool, then coarsely grind with 1 tsp sea salt. Dip warm bread first into olive oil, then into dukkah – divine.

tahini tomatoes In a blender, whiz 2 crushed garlic cloves with 1 tsp sea salt, 2 tbsp lemon juice, 3 tbsp tahini paste, 1/2 tsp ground cumin and 2 tbsp water. Add a little extra water until creamy. Drizzle over sliced tomatoes and scatter with mint.

spring onion tofu

Fresh or packaged beancurd (dofu in Cantonese, tofu in Japanese) is one of my favourite cool, no-cook dishes, because it so readily absorbs other flavours and looks so fresh with the wild, bright colours of spring onions and chilli.

SERVES 4

300 g silken Japanese tofu
4 spring onions (green
  part only)
1 large red chilli
1 tbsp sesame oil
1 tbsp soy sauce
2 tbsp coriander leaves

Gently remove the tofu from its packaging, and drain.

Cut the green spring onion stems into 5 cm lengths. Using the tip of a sharp knife, shred them lengthways into fine strips.

Trim the chilli top and bottom, cut in half and remove the seeds, then shred lengthways.

Cut the tofu into four equal blocks and arrange on a serving platter. Drizzle with sesame oil and soy. Toss the spring onions, chilli and coriander together and scatter on top.

Serve one each as a little appetiser, or serve as part of a Japanese or Chinese meal.

spinach & cheese quesadilla

Instant snack or excellent party food, quesadillas are fun to make, especially with wham-bam-pow gorgonzola melting inside. Find flour tortillas in the Mexican section at big supermarkets and ignore any instructions that say to fry in oil – they don't need it.

SERVES 4

500 g spinach leaves
sea salt and pepper
400 g fresh mozzarella balls
  (preferably buffalo), drained
200 g creamy blue cheese
  (eg gorgonzola)
8 wheat flour tortillas

Wash the spinach well and cook very briefly in a covered pan without extra water until wilted. Drain well, squeeze dry and finely chop. Add sea salt and pepper, and toss lightly.

Slice the mozzarella finely, and roughly crumble the blue cheese. Arrange some mozzarella slices over a flour tortilla, scatter with blue cheese and strew with spinach. Top with a second flour tortilla.

Transfer to a dry non-stick frying pan and cook over a medium heat for about 3 minutes until lightly browned. Turn once, and cook the other side until lightly browned and the cheese has melted.

Transfer to a board and keep warm, while you repeat with the remaining ingredients. Cut in half or into quarters and serve.

noodles

pasta

noodles

pasta

beef rice noodles

If you live near a Chinese food store look for fresh rice noodles, which have an incomparable slippery, soft texture. To use, pour boiling water over 500 g noodles, then drain and rinse under cold water before cooking.

SERVES 4

350 g rib eye or sirloin steak
2 tsp cornflour
1 tsp sesame oil
1 tbsp Chinese rice wine
4 tbsp soy sauce
200 g dried rice noodles
3 tbsp vegetable oil, plus
  extra for tossing noodles
1 sweet red pepper
4 spring onions
2 garlic cloves, finely sliced
2 cm knob of ginger, peeled
  and shredded
1 tbsp oyster sauce
1 tsp sugar
200 g bean sprouts, rinsed

Thinly slice the steak. Mix the cornflour with the sesame oil, then stir in the rice wine and 1 tbsp soy sauce. Toss the steak in this mixture and marinate for 30 minutes.

Add the dried noodles to a pan of boiling water and bring back to the boil, stirring. Cover and leave off the heat for 3 minutes, then drain and rinse under cold water. Toss in a little vegetable oil to prevent sticking.

Finely slice the pepper, discarding core and seeds. Slice the spring onions on the diagonal. Heat 2 tbsp oil in a wok, add the garlic, ginger, red pepper and most of the spring onions, and toss over high heat for 1 minute. Add the beef with its marinade and toss until coloured. Tip onto a warm plate.

Heat 1 tbsp oil in the wok, add the noodles and cook for 2 minutes over high heat. Add the remaining 3 tbsp soy sauce, 2 tbsp water, the oyster sauce, sugar and bean sprouts, tossing well, then add the beef and combine. Scatter with remaining spring onions and serve.

zucchini carbonara

The principle is the same as for *pasta alla carbonara*, but with courgettes instead of bacon: the heat of the freshly drained pasta cooks the eggs and cheese into a creamy golden sauce.

SERVES 2

200 g penne or fine tagliatelle
sea salt and coarsely ground
   black pepper
2 courgettes (zucchini), about
   250 g
3 egg yolks
40 g parmesan, freshly grated,
   plus extra for serving
1 tsp grated lemon zest

Cook the pasta in plenty of boiling, salted water for about 6 minutes until almost cooked. Meanwhile, trim the courgettes and cut lengthways into thick slices, then into strips and then into small dice.

Add the courgettes to the pasta water and cook for another 2 minutes until they are tender but not overly soft, and the pasta is *al dente*, tender but firm to the bite.

In a large bowl, beat the egg yolks, parmesan, lemon zest, sea salt and pepper together.

Drain the pasta and courgettes, reserving a few spoonfuls of the cooking water. Immediately add to the egg mixture, tossing quickly until the pasta is well coated. Add the reserved hot pasta water if dry, and toss again until lightly creamy.

Scatter with extra pepper and parmesan and serve in warm shallow bowls.

extra

no-cook pasta sauces

3 great recipes to serve 4:

ricotta & prosciutto

Mix 100 g ricotta cheese, 2 tbsp grated parmesan, 2 tbsp snipped chives and 4 torn prosciutto slices.

tomato & basil

Mix 4 peeled, deseeded and diced ripe tomatoes with 3 tbsp torn basil leaves, 3 tbsp extra virgin olive oil, 1 crushed garlic clove, sea salt and pepper.

lemon & parmesan

Mix 1 tbsp grated lemon zest with 2 tbsp grated parmesan, 2 tbsp roughly chopped parsley, 1 tbsp rinsed capers and 3 tbsp extra virgin olive oil.

to serve cook 400 g pasta until *al dente*. Drain, and toss while still very hot with your sauce.

bucatini with sardines

One of the tricks of good cooking is to use what is available and not to fuss too much about what isn't. Have confidence in your ability to turn a few stand-bys – canned sardines, pasta, capers, tomato passata and pine nuts – into something delicious, without compromising your own exquisite taste.

SERVES 4

400 g bucatini (fat spaghetti)
sea salt
1 tbsp olive oil
1 garlic clove, smashed
1 tbsp salted capers, rinsed
$1/2$ tsp dried chilli flakes or
  cayenne
2 anchovy fillets, chopped
300 ml passata or 400 g can
  tomatoes, drained and chopped
300 g can sardines or tuna,
  drained
1 tbsp pine nuts, toasted
1 tbsp roughly torn parsley

Cook the pasta in a large pan of simmering, salted water until *al dente*, tender but firm to the bite.

Meanwhile, heat the olive oil in a large frying pan over a low heat, and add the garlic, capers, chilli or cayenne, and anchovy fillets, stirring. Add the passata or canned tomatoes, stirring well, and simmer for 5 minutes.

When the pasta is almost ready, drain the sardines and roughly chop. Add to the sauce and gently heat through. Drain the pasta, reserving a few spoonfuls of the water, and add the pasta to the sauce, tossing well. If dry, add the reserved hot pasta water.

Scatter with the toasted pine nuts and torn parsley, and serve in warm pasta bowls.

angelhair with crab & lemon

This rich, but light pasta is also lovely with prawns. Fast cooking keeps the flavours fresh and light, so that even the tomato is still fresh tomato rather than tomato sauce.

SERVES 4

2 ripe tomatoes
300 g angelhair or tagliolini
    pasta (eg Cipriani)
sea salt and pepper
2 tbsp extra virgin olive oil,
    plus extra for serving
1 garlic clove, crushed
pinch of crushed dried chilli
1 tbsp salted capers, rinsed
3 tbsp dry white wine
300 g fresh cooked white
    crabmeat, picked over
1 tbsp lemon juice
2 tbsp chopped parsley
1 tbsp chopped basil
2 tsp finely grated lemon zest

Cut the tomatoes in half, squeeze out and discard the seeds and juice, then finely chop the flesh and set aside.

Cook the pasta in a large pan of boiling, salted water until *al dente*, tender but firm to the bite. (Very fine egg pasta will cook in just 2 minutes.)

Heat the olive oil in a frying pan. Add the garlic, chilli, capers and white wine, and cook for 1 minute, stirring.

Remove from the heat and add the chopped tomatoes, crabmeat, lemon juice, sea salt, pepper and most of the parsley and basil, stirring.

Drain the pasta well and add to the crab mixture, with an extra drizzle of olive oil, tossing well to coat.

Divide between four warm pasta plates, and scatter with the remaining herbs and grated lemon zest to serve.

soba noodles with tobiko

I always keep dried soba (buckwheat) noodles in the pantry for this refreshing, light, chilled noodle salad. Tobiko (pronounced *tob-ee-ko*) is crunchy, tiny flying fish roe, available from Japanese stores. You could also use salmon caviar.

SERVES 4

200 g dried buckwheat noodles
sea salt
1 tbsp lemon juice
1 tsp caster sugar
3 tbsp Japanese soy sauce
3 tbsp mirin
50 g tobiko or salmon caviar
1 tsp wasabi paste

Add the noodles to a large pan of boiling, salted water and cook for 6 to 8 minutes or until *al dente*, tender but still firm to the bite (as you would cook spaghetti). Drain well, rinse under cold running water, and chill for an hour or so.

Combine the lemon juice and sugar, stirring until the sugar has dissolved. Add the soy and mirin, stir, and chill for an hour or so.

When you are ready to serve, toss the noodles in the chilled sauce. Drain and toss with the tobiko, and divide between four chilled platters. Serve with wasabi paste, for those who like it hot.

tagliatelle with pumpkin & sage

This is a new look at Italy's lovely *tortelli di zucca*, which marries the natural sweetness of pumpkin with buttery, rich parmesan in an almost medieval manner. If your pumpkin is bland, use onion squash, butternut squash, or even sweet potato instead.

SERVES 4

600 g pumpkin

1 onion, peeled

3 tbsp butter

300 ml vegetable or chicken stock

1 tsp sugar

pinch of ground nutmeg

sea salt and pepper

300 g fine tagliatelle or fettuccine

1 tbsp olive oil

12 whole sage leaves, plus 6 roughly chopped leaves

4 tbsp freshly grated parmesan, plus extra for serving

Roughly chop the pumpkin, cut off the peel and seeds, and cut into 1 cm cubes. Halve and finely slice the onion.

Melt 2 tbsp butter in a frying pan, add the onion and cook gently for 5 minutes. Add the pumpkin and toss well, then add the stock, sugar, nutmeg and sea salt, and cook gently for 20 minutes or until tender. It should still be slightly soupy.

Add the pasta to a large pan of boiling, salted water and cook until *al dente*, tender but firm to the bite. Meanwhile, heat the olive oil in a small pan and gently fry the whole sage leaves until crisp.

Drain the pasta, and toss lightly with the pumpkin, adding the remaining 1 tbsp butter, chopped sage, parmesan and lots of pepper.

Divide between warm pasta bowls and scatter with the crisp sage leaves. Serve with extra parmesan at the table.

chicken & coriander salad

This is a favourite salad of mine whenever I come home with some cooked chicken or duck from Chinatown, or have some leftover chicken from a roast.

SERVES 4

1 carrot, peeled
1/2 cucumber, peeled
2 spring onions, trimmed
3 tbsp lime juice
1 tsp sugar
sea salt and pepper
1 shallot, peeled and finely
   sliced
250 g rice vermicelli noodles
2 cooked chicken breasts
1 tbsp sesame oil
1 tbsp fish sauce
3 tbsp coriander leaves
1/2 mild red chilli, finely sliced
2 tbsp roasted peanuts,
   chopped

Cut the carrot and cucumber into 10 cm sections, finely slice lengthways and then cut into fine matchsticks. Finely shred the spring onions lengthways.

Mix the lime juice with the sugar, sea salt and pepper. Toss the carrot, cucumber, spring onions and shallot in the mixture and set aside.

Pour boiling water over the noodles and leave to soak for 6 to 7 minutes. Roughly shred the cooked chicken.

Drain the noodles, rinse in cold water, and drain again. Snip 2 or 3 times with scissors, then toss with the chicken, sesame oil, fish sauce and coriander leaves. Add the chilli, shallot, spring onions, cucumber, carrot and lime dressing, and toss lightly.

Divide the salad between four serving bowls. Scatter with chopped peanuts and serve.

spaghetti al bianco

When Italians feel the need to look after themselves, they cook *'al bianco'*, 'white' food without the acidity of tomatoes. This lemon-scented 'white' meat ragu has the power to make us all feel better.

SERVES 4

10 g dried wild mushrooms
1 leek, trimmed
2 celery stalks
2 carrots, peeled
1 tbsp olive oil
1 tbsp butter
4 thyme sprigs
1 tbsp chopped parsley
750 g lean minced beef
1 tbsp plain flour
sea salt and pepper
500 ml hot stock or water
400 g spaghetti
1 tbsp grated lemon zest
freshly grated parmesan for
  serving

Soak the dried mushrooms in 250 ml boiling water for 30 minutes. Finely slice the leek and celery, and finely dice the carrots.

Heat the olive oil and butter in a pan and cook the leek for 5 minutes. Add the carrots, celery, thyme and parsley, and cook for 5 minutes. Add the beef and cook, stirring, until nicely browned. Scatter over the flour, sea salt and pepper, and stir for a minute or two to cook the flour.

Add the mushrooms with their soaking water, discarding any sediment. Gradually stir in the hot stock or water, then simmer, partly covered, for 45 minutes or longer.

Cook the spaghetti in plenty of boiling, salted water until *al dente*, tender but firm to the bite. Drain well, then toss with the meat sauce and add the grated lemon zest. Serve with freshly grated parmesan.

seafood

fish

seafood

fish

hangtown fry

This amazing omelette folded around crumbed, fried oysters was supposedly created during the Californian gold rush of 1849 for a miner who had struck it rich. I've freshened it up for a fun, quick supper. Serve with Tabasco on the side.

SERVES 2

4 streaky bacon rashers
6 – 8 large oysters, freshly
  opened
1 tbsp plain flour
sea salt and pepper
1 beaten egg for coating
2 tbsp fine dry breadcrumbs
2 tbsp butter
6 eggs, beaten
1 tbsp finely chopped parsley

Fry the bacon in a non-stick frying pan until crisp. Remove and set aside.

Reserve the oyster juices. Coat each oyster in flour, sea salt and pepper, then in the beaten egg, then in the breadcrumbs. Melt 1 tbsp butter in the pan and fry the oysters lightly until golden, turning once. Drain on kitchen paper and wipe the pan clean.

Beat the 6 eggs with the oyster juices, sea salt and pepper. Add the remaining 1 tbsp butter to the pan, pour in the eggs and stir briskly for 30 seconds.

Stop stirring and cook over medium heat, pulling back the edges as they set and tilting the pan to force the runny bits to the edges. When the omelette is almost set, add the oysters and parsley, and cook for a further 30 seconds.

Slide the omelette onto a warm plate, jerking the pan to help it fold in half. Serve half the omelette each, topped with the crisp bacon.

calamari with 'taramasalata'

A heavenly combination of paprika-dusted calamari rings with a light, fluffy purée of smoked salmon that tastes even better than traditional Greek taramasalata made with smoked cod's roe.

SERVES 4

500 g fresh squid (calamari), cleaned
100 g plain flour
$1/2$ tsp paprika
sea salt and pepper
3 tbsp olive oil
2 tbsp salmon roe

'TARAMASALATA'
100 g smoked salmon, chopped
200 g cream cheese
100 ml thick yoghurt
2 tsp horseradish cream
1 tbsp lemon juice

To make the 'taramasalata', combine the smoked salmon, cream cheese, yoghurt, horseradish cream, lemon juice and freshly ground pepper in a food processor. Whiz to combine, then refrigerate until required.

Cut the squid tubes into 1 cm rings, and the legs into smaller sections. Mix the flour with the paprika, 1 tsp salt and $1/2$ tsp pepper. Toss the squid pieces in the flour, then shake off the excess.

Heat half the olive oil in a frying pan until hot. Quickly fry the squid in batches, turning once, for about 30 seconds. Remove and drain on kitchen paper, adding a little extra oil to the pan for each batch.

Spoon the 'taramasalata' into four small pots and top with salmon roe. Serve with the fried calamari.

garlic sizzled prawns

There is normal food, and then there is holiday food. Holiday food in Spain means sitting in the sun drinking chilled white wine, nibbling on olives and bread, while you wait for the much-loved tapas dish of *gambas* (prawns) sizzled with the right amount of *ajillo* (garlic) and served in the still-sizzling pan.

SERVES 4

500 g raw prawns
sea salt and pepper
3 garlic cloves, crushed
1 small red chilli, chopped, or
    pinch of dried chilli flakes
$1/2$ tsp Spanish paprika
2 tbsp Spanish sherry
3 tbsp olive oil
1 tbsp torn parsley leaves

Peel the prawns, leaving the tails, and pat dry. Devein each prawn by threading a thin bamboo skewer through the back of the 'neck' and hooking out any black thread. Season with sea salt, and place the prawns in a small frying pan that you can take to the table.

Combine the crushed garlic, chilli, paprika, sherry and olive oil, and spoon over the prawns. Leave to marinate for 10 minutes or longer.

Place the frying pan over high heat and cook, shaking the pan to turn the prawns, for around 3 minutes, until they change colour and the garlic is lightly golden – the sherry will probably catch and flame, so be careful.

Scatter with parsley, sea salt and pepper, and serve while still sizzling, with plenty of bread to mop up the garlicky juices.

extra

garlicky, golden aïoli
A thick, lush, creamy mayonnaise, which adds a silky richness to anything it touches.

to make it whiz 2 egg yolks, 1 crushed garlic clove, ½tsp salt, 1tsp Dijon mustard, and 2tbsp lemon juice in a blender or processor. Very slowly, at a bare trickle, add 100ml sunflower or vegetable oil, then 100ml olive oil, whizzing until thick, smooth and silky. Beat in 1tbsp boiling water and refrigerate.

serve aïoli with garlicky prawns, seafood soups, grilled fish, asparagus, hard-boiled eggs, roast pork, tomato salads and vegetable stews.

salmon in light, fragrant broth

You can ruin the richness of salmon by teaming it with rich sauces, cream or mayonnaise. It doesn't need them. Instead, bathe it in a gentle, fragrant broth of Thai aromatics with a little kick of lime juice, and serve with steamed rice.

SERVES 4

4 salmon fillets, around
150 g each
3 tbsp fish sauce
2 lemongrass stalks, trimmed
2 shallots, peeled
1 small red chilli
150 g mushrooms (oyster,
shiitake or button)
100 g baby spinach leaves
500 ml chicken or vegetable
stock
1 tsp sugar
1 tbsp vegetable oil
sea salt and pepper
1 tbsp lime juice

Toss the salmon in 1 tbsp fish sauce and set aside. Peel the lemongrass stalks and finely slice the white part. Finely slice the shallots, chilli and mushrooms. Wash the spinach and drain.

Heat the stock in a saucepan with the lemongrass, shallots, chilli, mushrooms and sugar, and simmer for 10 minutes.

Heat the oil in a non-stick frying pan and sear the salmon, skin-side down, for 3 minutes or until the skin is crisp. Turn and lightly sear the other side for 1 minute, leaving the inside pink. Season with sea salt and pepper.

Add the spinach to the hot broth for 10 seconds until barely wilted, then remove with tongs. Divide the spinach among four warm, shallow bowls and place the salmon on top.

Add the remaining 2 tbsp fish sauce and the lime juice to the broth, and spoon it around the salmon. Serve with a bowl of rice to the side.

portuguese fish stew

This wet, soupy rice overflowing with fish, prawns and chorizo sausage is my favourite Portuguese holiday food. If you make it ahead, the rice will absorb the stock, so keep some extra stock handy and add it before serving.

SERVES 4

600 g thick, firm, white fish fillets, skinned
4 tbsp olive oil
8 raw prawns in shells
sea salt and pepper
2 chorizo sausages
1 sweet red pepper
1 onion, peeled
3 garlic cloves, finely chopped
2 large tomatoes, chopped
1.2 litres hot veg or fish stock
400 g risotto rice
1 tsp Spanish paprika
2 bay leaves
2 tbsp torn flat parsley leaves
1 lemon, quartered

Cut the fish into generous bite-sized pieces. Heat half the olive oil in a frying pan and cook the fish and prawns on all sides until they just change colour. Remove to a plate and season well.

Slice the chorizo sausages. Finely chop the red pepper, discarding the core and seeds. Halve and slice the onion. Heat the remaining olive oil in the pan and fry the onion, garlic, red pepper and chorizo slices for 10 minutes, stirring well.

Add the tomatoes and stock and bring to the boil. Add the rice, paprika, bay leaves, sea salt and pepper, stirring well. Reduce the heat to very low, then cover and simmer for 20 minutes until the rice is almost cooked, but still wet and soupy (add more stock if not).

Add the fish and prawns, and simmer gently for 10 minutes. Scatter with torn parsley and serve in warm pasta bowls, with lemon wedges for squeezing.

a bag of shellfish

This is a great way to cook up a mess of shellfish, the foil bag keeping all the flavour – and the nutrients – trapped inside. Make sure you have plenty of foil before you start, or you will get caught short.

SERVES 4

400 g clams
400 g mussels
12 raw prawns in shell, deveined
12 cherry tomatoes, halved
12 small black olives
1 red chilli, finely sliced
4 garlic cloves, flattened
4 tbsp extra virgin olive oil
1 tbsp chopped parsley
sea salt and pepper
1 lemon, quartered

Soak the clams and the mussels in cold water for an hour. Heat the oven to 230°C/Gas 8. To make the oven bags, cut four 45 cm long sheets of wide kitchen foil. Fold in half end to end, then crimp the sides together, leaving the top open.

Drain the mussels and clams. Scrub the mussels and pull out the little beards. Toss the prawns, clams and mussels in a big bowl with the cherry tomatoes, olives, chilli, garlic, olive oil, parsley, sea salt and pepper.

Divide the shellfish mixture between the four parcels. Seal the top by crimping tightly, so that no air can escape. Place on a roasting tray and bake for 15 minutes or until the bags puff up like balloons.

Carefully open and slide the contents and their juices onto a warm serving platter. Serve with lemon wedges, crusty bread and fingerbowls.

mexican baked fish

If you like pickled jalapeño chillies – and you're mad if you don't – then you'll love this fish, baked Veracruz style, under a rich sauce of onion, garlic, tomato, capers, olives and fiery jalapeños.

SERVES 4

4 thick, firm white fish fillets,
    180 g each, skinned
1 tbsp lime juice
$^1/_2$ tsp sea salt
1 onion, peeled
1 sweet red pepper
3 tbsp olive oil, plus extra
    for pan
1 garlic clove, finely sliced
400 g can tomatoes, chopped
10 green olives, pitted
1 tbsp salted capers, rinsed
1 tbsp pickled jalapeño chillies
pinch of cayenne pepper
1 bay leaf
coriander leaves for serving

Heat the oven to 200°C/Gas 6. Rub the fish with the lime juice and sea salt, and set aside.

Finely slice the onion into rings. Cut the red pepper into strips, discarding the core and seeds. Heat 2 tbsp olive oil in a frying pan and cook the onion for about 10 minutes until soft and pale. Add the garlic and cook for 1 minute.

Add the tomatoes, red pepper and 150 ml water, stirring. Add the green olives, capers, jalapeño chillies, cayenne and bay leaf. Cook gently for 10 to 15 minutes until the sweet red pepper is tender.

Heat 1 tbsp olive oil in a frying pan and sear the fish fillets for 1 minute on each side, then transfer to an oiled baking pan. Spoon the sauce on top and bake for 15 to 20 minutes until the fish is cooked through, depending on thickness. Scatter with coriander and serve with rice.

tamarind fish curry

What makes this simple fish curry special is the citrus tang of tamarind, extracted from the pulp of the tamarind pod. Find tamarind concentrate or purée in good supermarkets and Asian stores.

SERVES 4

700 g salmon fillets, skinned
1 tsp sea salt
1 onion, peeled
2 tbsp vegetable oil
1 garlic clove, crushed
2 cm knob of ginger, peeled
  and grated
1 tsp ground coriander
1 tsp ground cumin
$1/2$ tsp ground turmeric
2 small red chillies, sliced
1 tbsp tamarind concentrate
1 tbsp tomato purée (paste)
400 ml coconut milk
1 tsp sugar
torn coriander leaves to finish

Cut the salmon into bite-sized chunks. Rub with $1/2$ tsp salt and set aside.

Halve and finely slice the onion. Heat the oil in a heavy-based pan and fry the onion until soft but not coloured. Add the garlic and ginger, and fry for 1 minute, stirring.

Add the ground coriander, cumin, turmeric and chillies, stirring well until fragrant. Add the tamarind, tomato purée, coconut milk, 200 ml water, $1/2$ tsp salt and the sugar, and heat gently, stirring. Simmer, uncovered, for about 10 minutes. Taste and adjust for tamarind and chilli.

Add the fish and simmer for 5 minutes or until cooked. Scatter with coriander and serve with steamed rice.

lime

The lime is the exotic, tropical cousin of the everyday lemon – it's stronger, sweeter and more fashionable. For an instant lime sauce, add lime wedges to the roasting pan with chicken or lamb, or cook sliced limes alongside grilled or pan-fried fish – the limes soften and spill with warm tangy juices to make an instant sauce.

lime butter Blend 2 tbsp grated lime zest and 1/2 tsp sea salt into 100 g soft butter. Wrap in a bonbon of foil, twisting the ends tightly, and freeze for 1 hour. Unwrap, slice and serve on grilled or pan-fried fish.

avocado & lime whip Halve, stone and peel an avocado, then whiz in a food processor with 2 tbsp lime juice, a dash of Tabasco and sea salt until smooth. Spoon on top of rice crackers and top with lime zest.

pork with lime & mint In a wok, combine 300 g minced pork, 2 tbsp fish sauce, 1 finely sliced red chilli and 100 ml water. Cook for 10 minutes, stirring, until the water is absorbed. Add a squeeze of lime juice and a handful of mint leaves and serve in lettuce leaves.

cucumber & lime smash Cut 2 limes into quarters and pound to a pulp with 2 tbsp caster sugar. Divide between 2 tall glasses, add 50 ml vodka, finely sliced cucumber, mint leaves and crushed ice, then top up with tonic water.

lime & coconut macaroons Use your hands to mix 100 g caster sugar, 150 g desiccated coconut, 2 egg whites, 1 tbsp grated lime zest and 1 tbsp lime juice to a thick paste. Press into a flat square, 1 cm high. Cut out small rounds and bake on a tray at 170°C/Gas 3 for 12 to 15 minutes or until lightly golden.

salt baked fish

Sea bass is the classic choice, but this method is also brilliant with snapper, salmon, gurnard or any large, whole round-bodied fish. If your fish is larger than 1.3 kg, bake for 10 minutes per 500 g, plus an extra 10 minutes. And don't forget to show off the fish at the table before you crack open the salt crust.

SERVES 4

1 sea bass, around 1.3 kg, scaled and cleaned
3 rosemary sprigs
10 thyme sprigs
2 bay leaves
2 garlic cloves, smashed flat
4 egg whites
2 kg coarse or kosher sea salt
extra virgin olive oil for serving
1 lemon, quartered

Heat the oven to 180°C/Gas 4. Rinse the fish and pat dry. Stuff the rosemary, thyme, bay leaves and garlic into the cavity. Beat the egg whites until they form soft peaks, fold in the salt and mix well.

Lightly oil a non-stick baking sheet. Arrange half the salt mixture in a 1 cm layer across the middle, roughly to the same shape as the fish but a little wider. Place the fish on top. Pack the remaining salt mixture over the fish to cover it completely. Bake for 30 minutes until the crust has turned golden, then rest for 10 minutes.

Crack open the crust and gently transfer the fish to a warm large serving platter, brushing off any excess salt. Peel off any skin (sometimes it lifts off with the crust), and serve the fish with a drizzle of extra virgin olive oil and lemon wedges.

chicken

pork

chicken

pork

turkey with chorizo & lemon

The ultimate celebration package for everything from a birthday buffet dinner to Christmas Day: a golden, roasted breast of turkey rolled around a stuffing of spicy chorizo sausage, lemon and herbs.

SERVES 6

300 g fresh chorizo sausages
1 turkey breast fillet,
  around 1.3 kg
sea salt and pepper
1 tbsp finely grated lemon zest
50 g parmesan, freshly grated
$1/2$ tsp freshly grated nutmeg
1 tbsp finely chopped parsley
1 tbsp finely chopped thyme
1 egg, beaten
100 g fresh white breadcrumbs
1 lemon, sliced
400 ml dry white wine, stock
  or water

To make the stuffing, skin the chorizo sausages. Pinch the meat into a frying pan and cook for 5 minutes, then cool. Heat oven to 200°C/Gas 6.

To butterfly the turkey breast, lay skin-side down on a board and make a shallow cut down the centre of the meat, then cut horizontally through the thick meat to either side and open it up like a book. Cover with plastic film and bash it flat with a rolling pin, then rub with sea salt and pepper.

Lightly mix the cooled chorizo with the lemon zest, parmesan, nutmeg, parsley, thyme, egg and breadcrumbs.

Form the stuffing into a sausage on top of the turkey. Roll tightly, tuck in the ends and tie securely with string. Season well.

Place the turkey roll, skin-side up, in a roasting pan and arrange the lemon slices on top. Add the wine to the pan and roast for 1 hour and 10 minutes. Rest for 10 minutes, then remove the string and carve thickly. Serve with the cooking juices.

bang bang chicken

Why bang bang? Apparently, Sichuan street vendors sold this as a snack, first hammering the chicken with a 'bang' or wooden cudgel to loosen the fibres.

SERVES 4

2 chicken breasts
2 slices peeled fresh ginger
4 spring onions, trimmed
$1/2$ cucumber, peeled
1 carrot, peeled
2 celery stalks
1 tsp sesame oil
1 tsp rice wine vinegar
1 tsp sesame seeds, toasted

SAUCE

1 tbsp sesame oil
2 tbsp peanut butter
1 tbsp sweet chilli sauce
2 tbsp soy sauce
2 tsp caster sugar
1 tbsp rice wine vinegar
1 small red chilli, finely sliced

Put the chicken into a pan with 1 tsp salt, the ginger and enough cold water to cover. Finely shred the spring onions and add half to the pan. Bring to a simmer and poach gently for 15 minutes. Turn off the heat and leave for 30 minutes, then drain.

Cut the cucumber, carrot and celery into matchsticks. Finely shred the chicken and combine with the cucumber, carrot, celery and remaining spring onions. Add the sesame oil and vinegar, sea salt and pepper, and toss to mix. Arrange in four bowls or platters.

To make the sauce, mix the sesame oil, peanut butter, chilli sauce, soy, sugar, vinegar and sliced chilli until you have a paste. Gradually whisk in up to 100 ml water until runny but still quite thick.

Spoon the sauce over the chicken and vegetables, scatter with toasted sesame seeds and serve, with chopsticks.

honey

Golden, luscious honey makes everyone's lives that little bit sweeter. Like wines, there are honey varietals, made from single flowers as opposed to blends, so find the ones you like and use different honeys for different reasons. To measure honey, use a honey twirler, or dip your spoon in hot water first, and the honey will slip and slide off the spoon easily.

honey figs Halve 4 figs, lay on foil and drizzle with 1 tbsp honey. Grill for 5 minutes and serve with a creamy blue cheese and oat biscuits.

honey roast pork Cut 500 g pork fillet into 15 cm lengths. Marinate in 2 tbsp honey, 2 tbsp hoisin sauce, 2 tbsp soy sauce and $1/2$ tsp five-spice powder for 1 hour. Roast on a rack set over a tray of water at 220°C/Gas 7 for 30 minutes, basting occasionally. Slice and serve with rice or noodles, or toss in a stir-fry.

honey sausages Roast your favourite pork sausages until crisp-skinned. Drizzle with 2 tbsp honey and a squeeze of lemon juice. Amazing.

honey, ginger & lemon tea To ease a sore throat, put a slice of fresh ginger, a slice of lemon and 1 tbsp honey in a heatproof glass and pour boiling water over. Stir and sip.

honey lassi Whiz 150 g mixed berries and 1 tbsp honey in a blender until smooth, and spoon into chilled glasses. Whiz 200 g yoghurt, 2 tbsp honey and 6 ice cubes, pour on top and gently stir.

honey roast pears Heat 2 tbsp butter with 2 tbsp honey in a frying pan, stirring. Peel and halve 2 pears and pan-roast, spooning the sauce over the pears until caramelised. Serve with a glass of dessert wine.

maple roast pork

This is a typically gutsy, clever 'gastropub' recipe, adapted from a recipe by chef Steve Harris of The Sportsman pub near Whitstable on the English coast.

SERVES 4

1 tbsp smoked paprika
4 tbsp maple syrup
3 tbsp vegetable oil
4 large pork loin chops,
   about 250 g each
2 tbsp mayonnaise
1 tbsp grainy mustard
250 g greens or spinach
sea salt and pepper
1 tbsp butter
squeeze of lemon juice

Mix the paprika, maple syrup and 2 tbsp of the oil together in a bowl, then rub into the pork chops. Cover and refrigerate for as long as you have, be it an hour or overnight.

Heat the oven to 170°C/Gas 3. Heat the remaining oil in a frying pan, and gently pan-fry each chop on both sides, until it starts to blacken. (Be careful, as the rendered fat might spit.) Using tongs, hold the chop at right angles to the pan to colour the strip of fat as well, then transfer to a baking dish. Cook the chops in the oven for 25 minutes until tender.

Mix the mayonnaise and mustard together and set aside.

Wash and dry the greens and shred finely. Cook in a little boiling, salted water until tender, then drain thoroughly. Dress with the butter, lemon juice, and sea salt and pepper to taste.

Spoon the cooking juices over the chops and season well. Serve with the greens and mustard mayonnaise.

claypot chicken

This is my magic marinade – magic, because whatever meat is left in it becomes magically tender. Traditionally this would have been cooked in a claypot, but you can use any sort of pot or pan.

SERVES 4

10 dried black mushrooms
  (shiitake)
500 g boneless chicken thighs
100 g canned bamboo shoots
4 spring onions, trimmed
300 g firm tofu, drained
2 thick slices of peeled ginger
2 tbsp vegetable oil
1 tbsp Chinese rice wine
2 tbsp soy sauce
1 tsp sugar
2 tsp cornflour

MAGIC MARINADE:

2 tbsp soy sauce
1 tsp sesame oil
1 tsp cornflour

Soak the mushrooms in 250 ml boiling water for 30 minutes. Cut the chicken into generous bite-sized pieces. For the marinade, combine the soy, sesame oil and cornflour in a bowl. Add the chicken, turn to coat and marinate for 20 minutes.

Drain the mushrooms, reserving 200 ml water, and finely slice, discarding stems. Finely slice the bamboo shoots. Cut the spring onions on the diagonal into 5 cm lengths. Cut the tofu into 2 cm cubes. Cut the ginger into matchsticks.

Heat the oil in a wok or wide cooking pot, and stir-fry the ginger and chicken for 2 minutes. Add the mushrooms, bamboo shoots and spring onions, and stir-fry for 2 minutes. Add the mushroom water, rice wine, soy and sugar, and bring to the boil. Add the tofu and simmer for 15 minutes.

Mix the 2 tsp cornflour with 1 tbsp cold water and add to the wok, stirring well until the sauce thickens. Serve with rice.

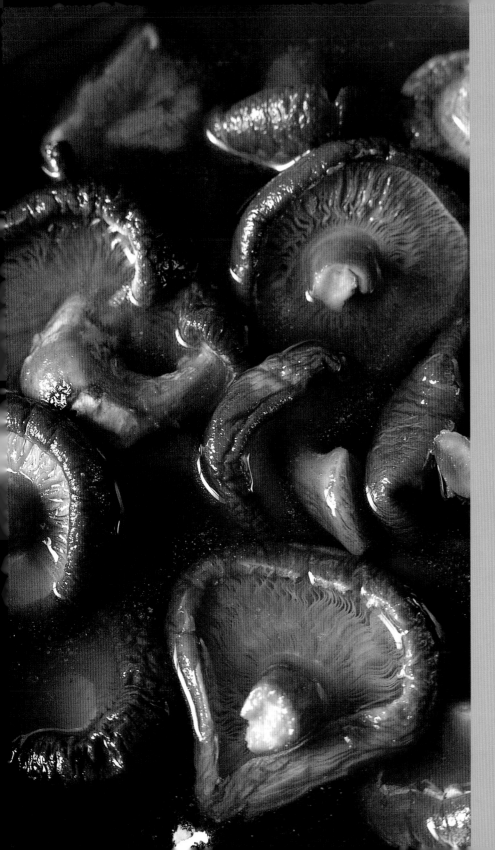

extra

dried mushrooms
With a pack of dried black (shiitake) mushrooms, you are just a soak away from great stocks and sauces.

mushroom stock
Soak 6 dried mushrooms in 250 ml boiling water for 30 minutes. Pick out the mushrooms and slice finely, discarding stems. Strain stock through a fine sieve. Use stock and mushrooms in soups, stir-fries, risotto and sauces.

shiitake sauce
Heat the sliced mushrooms and their stock with 1 tbsp each soy, hoisin and oyster sauces. Mix 2 tsp cornflour and 1 tbsp Chinese rice wine to a smooth paste and stir into the mushroom mixture. Simmer, stirring, until it thickens. Serve spooned over pan-fried pork, fish or chicken.

grilled pork balls with mint

Vietnamese cooking is light, fresh and healthy, and, as its defining characteristic, uses basket-loads of fresh herbs and salad greens. These meatballs (*nem nuong*) are typically light and lovely.

SERVES 4

1 tbsp Thai fragrant or jasmine rice (raw, not washed)

400 g minced pork

2 garlic cloves, crushed

sea salt and pepper

1 tbsp fish sauce

1 tbsp caster sugar

250 g dried rice vermicelli

2 tbsp mint leaves

1 iceberg lettuce, chilled

DRESSING

1 tsp caster sugar

2 tbsp lime juice

3 tbsp fish sauce

2 tbsp chopped mint

1 red or green chilli, sliced

Presoak 8 bamboo skewers in water to prevent them burning. Dry-fry the rice in a small frying pan until lightly golden, then grind to a powder.

Combine the pork, ground rice, garlic, $1/2$ tsp sea salt, $1/4$ tsp pepper, fish sauce and sugar, and knead until well mixed. With wet hands, shape the mixture into around 24 small balls, the size of a walnut.

Cook the noodles in boiling water for 2 to 3 minutes until just cooked, drain and rinse in cold water.

To make the dressing, mix the sugar with the lime juice, then add the fish sauce, mint and chilli. Toss the drained noodles in the dressing.

Heat the grill. Drain the skewers and thread the pork balls onto them, three to a skewer. Grill, turning occasionally, for 5 minutes until golden brown. Serve with the noodle salad, extra mint leaves, and lettuce leaves for wrapping.

provençal garlic chicken

This is the ultimate garlic dish, based on the classic pot-roasted chicken with forty cloves of garlic. Serve with a small leaf and herb salad, with a spoonful of the cooking juices whisked into the vinaigrette.

SERVES 4

1 oven-ready organic chicken, around 1.5 kg
sea salt and pepper
2 bay leaves
few thyme sprigs
4 tbsp olive oil, plus extra for casserole
40 plump whole garlic cloves, unpeeled
8 or 12 small new potatoes, unpeeled
75 ml dry white wine

Heat the oven to 180°C/Gas 4. Rub the chicken with a little salt, pop the bay leaves and 2 thyme sprigs inside, and truss with string.

Place in a lightly oiled, large, lidded casserole and add the garlic cloves, potatoes and white wine. Drizzle the olive oil over the chicken, scatter a few thyme sprigs over and season well with sea salt and pepper.

Lay a sheet of foil across the casserole, clamp the lid on tightly and bake for 1 hour and 15 minutes. Remove the lid, increase the heat to 220°C/Gas 7 and cook for a further 10 or 15 minutes until the skin is golden and the chicken is cooked through.

Gently transfer the chicken to a serving platter, remove the string and carve. Pile the garlic cloves on top of the chicken and serve with the potatoes and cooking juices. Squish the garlic and eat the sweet nutty purée with the chicken.

mustard chicken wings

Mustard, honey and lemon juice combine to give chicken wings a golden suntan and a real flavour kick. Serve as an easy, no-fuss, lunch or supper, or cool and pack for a picnic.

SERVES 4

8 chicken wings
1 tbsp honey
2 tbsp Dijon mustard
2 tsp lemon juice
sea salt and pepper
2 bunches watercress
1 orange
4 crisp baby radishes
1 tsp olive oil
1 tbsp balsamic vinegar

Trim the chicken wings and pat dry. Mix the honey, mustard, lemon juice, sea salt and pepper in a bowl, and toss the wings well until coated. Leave to marinate for 30 minutes.

Heat the oven to 200°C/Gas 6. Place the chicken wings on a rack set above a foil-lined tray (to help stop the drips from burning) and bake for 30 minutes or until sticky and golden.

Meanwhile, trim the watercress, wash and spin dry. Peel the orange thickly, removing the white pith, and cut into segments. Finely slice the radishes. Toss the watercress, orange and radishes in the olive oil and balsamic vinegar.

Serve the hot chicken wings with the orange and watercress salad.

chinese spare ribs

If it's summer, you can toss these on the barbecue. If it isn't, then cook them in the oven, and they will still end up gloriously caramelised and sticky. To turn them into a meal, serve with rice and Chinese greens.

SERVES 4

1 kg long pork spare ribs

MARINADE

2 tsp Chinese five-spice powder

150 g hoisin sauce

2 tbsp tomato ketchup

3 tbsp Chinese rice wine or dry sherry

$1/2$ tsp sea salt

1 tbsp freshly grated ginger

DIPPING SAUCE

2 tbsp hoisin sauce

1 tbsp sweet chilli sauce

1 tbsp soy sauce

For the marinade, combine the five-spice powder, hoisin, ketchup, rice wine, salt and ginger in a bowl and mix thoroughly. Cut the pork into individual ribs, add to the marinade and turn to coat thoroughly. Leave to marinate for 2 hours or overnight, tossing occasionally.

Heat the oven to 230°C/Gas 8. Place the ribs on a wire rack set over a baking tray containing 250 ml water. Bake for 20 minutes, then turn the ribs over, lower the oven setting to 200°C/Gas 6 and cook for a further 15 to 20 minutes. Keep an eye on them – you want them scorched and sizzling, but not burnt to a frazzle.

For the dipping sauce, combine the hoisin, sweet chilli and soy sauces. Remove the spare ribs from the oven and serve with the dipping sauce.

lamb

beef

lamb

beef

beef & beer stew

This wonderfully rich stew is based on the famous Flemish carbonnade, of beef braised in beer with plenty of onions. The secret is to brown your meat really well to begin with.

SERVES 4 TO 6

1 kg beef shoulder (chuck)
2 tbsp plain flour
sea salt and pepper
600 g small white onions
2 tbsp olive oil
2 tbsp butter
1 tbsp tomato purée (paste)
2 bay leaves
1 tbsp Dijon mustard
1 tbsp soft brown sugar
400 ml beer (preferably lager)
300 ml boiling stock or water
2 tbsp torn flat parsley leaves

Heat the oven to 150°C/Gas 2. Cut the beef into large cubes, about 50 g each, and coat lightly in the flour, sea salt and pepper. Peel the onions, keeping the root, then cut through the root into thick wedges.

Heat half the oil and butter in a large flameproof casserole and brown the meat in batches, on all sides, removing to a plate when browned.

Add the remaining oil and butter to the casserole and cook the onions for 10 minutes until soft. Add the tomato purée, bay leaves, mustard, sugar, salt and pepper, stirring. Gradually add the beer, stirring constantly, then the boiling stock or water.

Return the beef to the casserole and bring to a simmer. Cover and cook in the oven (or gently on the hob if you prefer), stirring occasionally, for 2$\frac{1}{2}$ to 3 hours. Scatter with parsley and serve with mashed potato and something green.

lamb rump & spring onion mash

This is a brilliant mini-roast. Ask for boned lamb rumps, or chumps, and count on around 200 g meat per person, or three smaller or two larger rumps to serve four.

SERVES 4

4–6 anchovy fillets
4 x 200 g or 3 x 300 g boned
   lamb rumps (chumps)
sea salt and pepper
a little olive oil
200 g cherry tomatoes
SPRING ONION MASH
600 g potatoes, peeled
1 tbsp butter
6 spring onions, finely chopped
60 ml milk
freshly grated nutmeg

Heat the oven to 220°C/Gas 7. Arrange the anchovy fillets on the 'inside' of each rump, season well, roll up and tie into shape with string. Brush with olive oil and sear in a hot pan until well browned all over.

Toss the cherry tomatoes in olive oil, place in a roasting pan and roast for 10 minutes. Add the lamb to the roasting pan and roast, allowing 15 minutes for 200 g rumps, or 20 minutes for 300 g rumps, for medium rare meat, removing the tomatoes when soft and squishy.

Meanwhile, cut the potatoes into chunks and cook in boiling, salted water until tender, about 20 minutes.

Rest the lamb for 10 minutes under a loose sheet of foil. Drain the potatoes, add the butter and mash. Beat in the spring onions, milk and grated nutmeg, sea salt and pepper to taste.

Remove the string and thickly slice the lamb. Serve with the spring onion mash and roasted tomatoes, and drizzle with the roasting juices.

fast greek lamb with feta

Marinate your lamb in garlic, oregano, lemon juice and olive oil, then quickly sear until hot and scorchy. Wrap it in warm pitta bread with yoghurt and feta, and serve with lemon wedges and a cold beer.

SERVES 4

750 g lamb loin, fillets or
  leg steaks
1 tsp dried oregano
1 tbsp thyme leaves
4 rounds pitta bread
4 tbsp thick Greek-style
  yoghurt
100 g feta cheese, crumbled
1 lemon, quartered
MARINADE
2 garlic cloves, crushed
2 tbsp olive oil
$1/2$ tsp dried oregano
1 tbsp lemon juice
sea salt and pepper

Slice the lamb finely but roughly, at different angles (basically, hack it to bits). For the marinade, combine the garlic, olive oil, oregano, lemon juice, sea salt and pepper in a bowl. Add the lamb, turn to coat and leave to marinate until ready to cook.

Heat a non-stick frying pan and sear the lamb over a high heat, tossing it in the pan until crisped on the edges, but still a little pink inside. Add the oregano and thyme, and toss well.

Heat the pitta bread in a warm oven or dry frying pan for 3 minutes, and place a pitta on each plate. Add a spoonful of yoghurt, pile the lamb on top and scatter the feta over. Serve with lemon quarters for squeezing.

roast peppered beef

The dinner party classic returns, this time with a peppery crust and a light red wine and horseradish sauce. Beautiful beef like this is worth the expense – and worth cracking open a great bottle of red.

SERVES 6 TO 8

1 prime beef fillet, around
  1.8 kg
1 tbsp plain flour
2 tbsp Dijon mustard
sea salt
1 tbsp cracked black pepper
a little olive oil for the pan
100 ml red wine
100 ml chicken stock
1 tbsp horseradish sauce
1 tbsp cold butter, diced
2 bunches of watercress,
  washed

Heat the oven to 230°C/Gas 8. Tuck in the tail end of the beef and tie with string to keep an even shape. Mix the flour, mustard and 1/2 tsp sea salt together to a paste, and spread over the beef with your hands. Scatter with cracked pepper.

Place the beef fillet in an oiled roasting pan and roast for 15 minutes, then reduce the heat to 200°C/Gas 6 and roast for a further 15 minutes per kg, for rare to medium rare meat. Transfer the beef to a warm plate, cover loosely with foil and rest for 15 minutes while you make the sauce.

Put the roasting pan on the hob over a medium heat. Add the wine and bring to the boil, scraping up any beefy juices. Add the stock and bring to the boil. Strain into a small pan and add any juices from the beef. Whisk in the horseradish sauce, butter and sea salt to taste, and keep warm.

Carve the beef thickly and arrange on six warm dinner plates with the watercress. Serve with the red wine and horseradish sauce.

extra

rare roast beef
Turn your leftover beef into world-class eating.

beef rolls with daikon
Top 10 slices of rare roast beef with grated daikon (Chinese white radish). Roll up, drizzle with sesame oil and scatter with Japanese togarashi pepper.

rare beef tonnata
Whiz 125 g good tuna with 3 anchovy fillets, 1 tbsp lemon juice, 1 tbsp rinsed salted capers and 150 ml mayonnaise. Drizzle over thinly sliced roast beef.

thai beef salad
Mix together 2 tbsp lime juice, 2 tbsp Thai fish sauce, 1 tsp caster sugar and 1 tsp sesame oil. Toss with strips of rare roast beef and lots of basil, mint and coriander leaves.

steak tartare burgers

Take the ingredients of the traditional raw steak tartare, mix them up with your hands, form into burgers and sear in a pan until crusty, and as rare as you dare.

SERVES 2

400 g best quality minced beef

1 egg yolk, beaten

3 anchovy fillets, chopped

1 shallot, peeled and finely minced

2 cornichons or cocktail gherkins, finely chopped

2 tsp salted capers, rinsed

1 tsp Dijon mustard

dash of Tabasco

1 tbsp chopped parsley

sea salt and pepper

1 tbsp olive oil

2 fresh English muffins

few rocket leaves for serving

In a bowl, combine the minced beef with the egg yolk, anchovy fillets, shallot, cornichons, capers, mustard, Tabasco, parsley, sea salt and pepper, mixing and mulching it well with your hands.

Shape the meat into two large, thick, round patties. Heat the olive oil in a frying pan and sear the burgers on one side for 4 minutes until dark and crusty, then turn and cook the other side briefly, keeping it as rare as you dare.

Heat the grill. Split the muffins and toast lightly under the grill. Place each burger on a muffin base, top with a few rocket leaves and lean the muffin top against it. Serve Dijon mustard or tomato ketchup on the side.

moorish lamb shanks

Long, slow cooking on the bone means meltingly tender meat in a rich, spicy, saffron-scented, Spanish-inspired stew.

SERVES 4

2 onions, peeled
4 carrots, peeled
2 celery stalks
4 lamb shanks, well trimmed
sea salt and pepper
flour for dusting
2 tbsp olive oil
250 ml dry white wine
1 tsp Spanish smoked paprika
good pinch of saffron powder
2 tbsp tomato purée (paste)
400 g can chopped tomatoes
1 sweet red pepper
400 g can chickpeas, drained
1 tbsp torn flat parsley leaves

Roughly chop the onions and carrots, and slice the celery. Dust the lamb shanks in seasoned flour.

Heat the olive oil in a large lidded frying pan or flameproof casserole. Add the lamb shanks and brown well on all sides, then remove to a plate.

Add the onions, carrots and celery to the pan and cook, moving them around occasionally, for 10 minutes until they start to soften. Add the wine and let it bubble and evaporate. Add the paprika, saffron, tomato purée, tomatoes and 1 tsp salt, stirring well.

Return the lamb shanks to the pan, and add enough water to almost cover the bones. Cover and simmer gently for 1 hour.

Roughly chop the red pepper, discarding the core and seeds. Add to the pan with the chickpeas and cook for another 1 hour or until the lamb shanks are tender and the whole thing is stewy rather than soupy. Taste for salt and pepper, scatter with parsley leaves and serve.

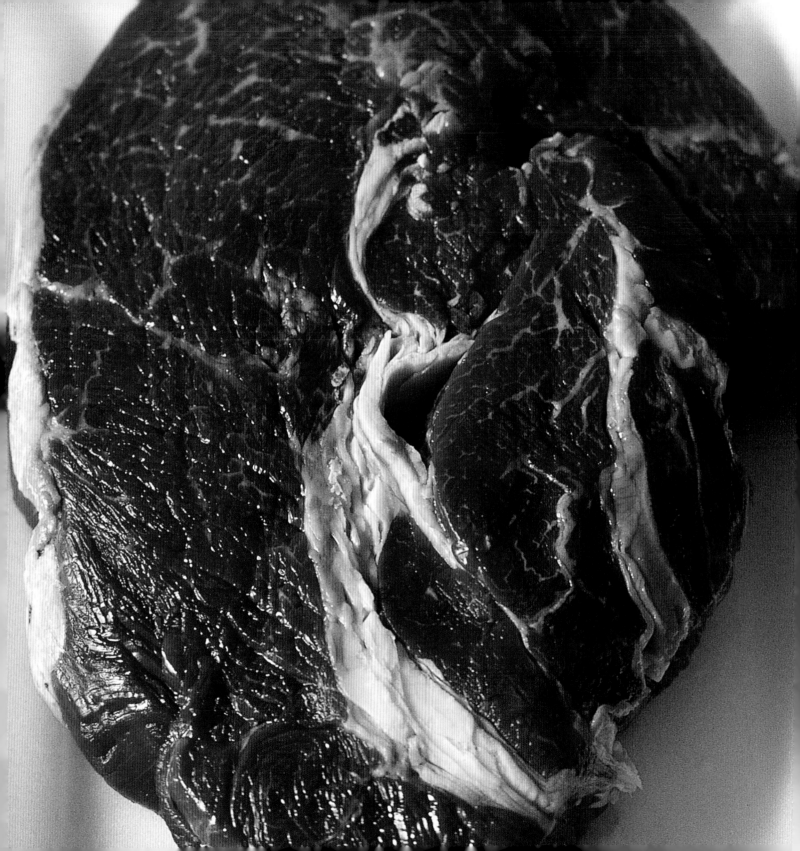

new york meatloaf

How clever is this – a hand-formed meatloaf that comes with a built-in tomato sauce. Serve hot, or cool and serve in huge bread rolls for lunch.

SERVES 4

4 slices bread, crusts removed
100 ml milk
1 leek, trimmed
1 sweet red pepper
500 g minced beef
250 g good sausage mince
2 tbsp finely chopped parsley
sea salt and pepper
$1/2$ tsp cayenne pepper
$1/4$ tsp ground nutmeg
2 tbsp tomato ketchup
2 tsp Worcestershire sauce
  or Dijon mustard
1 egg, beaten
400 g can chopped tomatoes
6 cherry tomatoes, halved
$1/2$ tsp dried oregano

Heat the oven to 200°C/Gas 6. Soak the bread in the milk for a minute or two, then lightly squeeze dry. Very finely chop the leek. Finely chop the red pepper, discarding the core and seeds.

Combine the bread, beef, sausage, leek, red pepper, parsley, sea salt, pepper, cayenne, nutmeg, ketchup and Worcestershire sauce in a large bowl. Knead with your hands until well mixed, then add the beaten egg and squish well until a little gluey. Shape the mixture into a loaf shape with your hands.

Place the meatloaf in a roasting pan lined with greaseproof paper. Strew the chopped tomatoes and cherry tomatoes along the top and scatter with sea salt, pepper and oregano. Bake for 1 hour or until cooked through.

Slice the meatloaf thickly and serve with green beans or watercress.

anchovy

Salt-cured anchovies in oil are a life-saver in the kitchen, injecting character and charm. Look for large, plump, fleshy anchovies from the Cantabrian sea of Spain (eg Ortiz) and put them to work on meats, vegetables, salads and pizzas.

anchovy bruschetta Rub cut tomatoes over a split baguette, squeezing out the flesh and juices. Brush with garlicky olive oil, and grill until scorchy. Top with anchovy fillets and serve with drinks.

tapenade Whiz 200 g pitted black olives with 100 g drained tuna in oil, 4 anchovy fillets, 1 tbsp rinsed capers, a pinch of dried chilli flakes, 1 tbsp Dijon mustard, 1 tbsp lemon juice and pepper, in a blender. Gradually blend in 3 tbsp extra virgin olive oil to make a rich, dark paste. Serve on halved cherry tomatoes.

anchovy chilli butter Soften 150 g butter and fold in 10 chopped anchovy fillets, 2 finely chopped red chillies and 1 crushed garlic clove. Serve with grilled steaks or steamed veggies.

anchovy roast lamb Cut 16 slits in a leg of lamb. Push $1/2$ anchovy or a rosemary sprig into each, pour oil from the anchovy can over, and roast at 200°C/Gas 6 until done to your liking.

anchoiade Pound 24 anchovy fillets with 2 tbsp tomato purée (paste) and 2 garlic cloves. Beat in 4 tbsp extra virgin olive oil, 1 tbsp orange juice and pepper. Spoon onto hard-boiled quail eggs.

anchovy, lemon & parmesan dressing Whiz 2 crushed garlic cloves, 3 anchovy fillets, 1 tsp Dijon mustard, 1 tsp sugar, 1 tbsp lemon juice, 1 tbsp grated parmesan, sea salt and pepper until smooth. Slowly blend in 100 ml light olive oil. Drizzle over lettuce leaves.

lamb chop curry

This spice mix is as close as I can get to a good old-fashioned curry powder, the sort we loved before we started grinding our own spices.

SERVES 4

100 g yoghurt
sea salt
8 well-trimmed lamb cutlets
1 onion, peeled
2 tbsp vegetable oil
1 tbsp grated fresh ginger
2 garlic cloves, crushed
1 tbsp tomato purée (paste)
200 g peas (fresh or frozen)
SPICE MIX
1/2 tsp each ground coriander, cumin, fenugreek, ginger, black pepper, cayenne and turmeric

For the spice mix, combine all the spices in a bowl and stir well. Mix 1 tsp of this curry powder with the yoghurt and 1 tsp sea salt. Toss the lamb cutlets in the spiced yoghurt until lightly coated.

Halve and slice the onion. Heat the oil in a frying pan and cook the onion for 10 minutes until soft. Add the ginger, garlic and remaining curry powder, stirring. Add the lamb chops and their marinade and brown lightly, turning once.

Add the tomato purée and 400 ml water, bring to a simmer and cook gently, uncovered, for 30 to 40 minutes or until the lamb is tender and the sauce has thickened.

Cook the peas in simmering, salted water for 5 minutes or until tender, then drain and add to the curry. Serve with rice.

chocolate

fruit

chocolate

fruit

rosy peaches with basil

Peaches are so perfect they need very little to make them extra special – just a quick poach in basil-scented rosé wine and a few adoring strawberries.

SERVES 4

4 unblemished, ripe peaches
150 g caster sugar
10 basil leaves, plus extra
  for serving
400 ml rosé wine
1 small punnet strawberries

To peel the peaches, lightly score the skin from top to bottom and dunk them in a pan of simmering water for 10 seconds. Remove and peel under cold running water.

Combine the sugar, basil leaves and rosé wine in a small saucepan, and bring to the boil, stirring. Tuck in the peaches and poach gently for 5 to 10 minutes, depending on ripeness. Gently remove the peaches.

Boil the syrup briskly until it is syrupy. Set aside to cool, then strain. Wash the strawberries but do not hull.

To serve, drizzle the peaches with the rosé syrup. Coat the strawberries in the syrup and arrange them next to the peaches. Scatter with a few fresh basil leaves.

chocolate honeycomb crêpes

Seductively dark chocolate crêpes are topped with crunchy honeycomb and yoghurt. If you can't find confectionery honeycomb, crunch up a chocolate-coated honeycomb bar or a couple of sesame snaps and scatter on top.

SERVES 4

100 g plain flour
20 g cocoa powder, plus
　extra for dusting
3 tbsp honey
pinch of salt
2 medium eggs
150 ml milk
50 g confectionery honeycomb
50 g plain chocolate
4 tsp butter
100 g Greek-style yoghurt,
　chilled
1 tsp icing sugar for dusting

To make the crêpe batter, blend the flour, cocoa powder, honey, salt, eggs and milk in a food processor until smooth and creamy. Rest the batter in the fridge for at least 30 minutes.

Roughly chop the honeycomb and set aside. Melt the chocolate in a heatproof bowl set over a pan of simmering water, and keep warm.

Melt 1 tsp butter in a crêpe pan or small non-stick frying pan over a medium heat. Add a ladleful of batter and swirl to cover the base thinly. Cook for a minute or two until set on top, then turn and briefly cook the other side. Keep warm while you cook the remaining crêpes, adding 1 tsp butter to the pan each time.

Serve the crêpes on warm plates, folded, rolled, or loosely draped. Top with a dollop of yoghurt and dust with cocoa powder sifted with the icing sugar. Scatter with honeycomb and drizzle with the melted chocolate.

chocolate cashew mousse

This is a Mexican take on everyone's favourite choccy mousse, combining chocolate with cashews, and infusing the chocolate with dried chilli for a tingling warmth that comes through the richness.

SERVES 4

100 g dark, bitter chocolate
1/2 tsp dried chilli flakes
1/2 tsp ground cinnamon
25 g roasted salted cashews, plus 4 extra to finish
3 medium eggs, separated
4 tbsp honey

Roughly chop the chocolate and place in a heatproof bowl set over a pan of simmering water. As soon as it starts to melt, add the dried chilli and cinnamon, take the pan off the heat, and stir until smooth. Allow to cool for 10 minutes.

Whiz the cashews in a blender or food processor until finely ground. Beat the egg yolks and honey in a bowl until smooth. Stir in the chocolate and ground cashews until smooth.

Beat the egg whites in a clean bowl until they form soft peaks, and gently fold into the chocolate mixture.

Spoon into four small pots and chill for 2 hours. To serve, top each mousse with a whole salted cashew.

extra

chocolate infusions
Add something more exciting than vanilla when you melt chocolate for brownies, puddings, sauces and icings.

chilli chocolate Infuse 100 g melted chocolate with 1 finely sliced, deseeded small red chilli.

ginger chocolate Infuse 100 g melted chocolate with 1 tbsp chopped preserved stem ginger.

sea salt & pepper chocolate Infuse 100 g melted chocolate with $1/2$ tsp sea salt and $1/2$ tsp ground black pepper.

mayan chocolate Infuse 100 g melted chocolate with $1/2$ tsp ground cinnamon, $1/2$ tsp ground allspice and a good grating of nutmeg.

vienna plum cake

A gloriously old-fashioned mittel-European cake that brings back memories of Viennese coffeehouses. Serve warm as a pudding, or cool and serve as a cake.

180 g butter, softened, plus extra for tin
160 g caster sugar
4 medium eggs
$1/2$ tsp pure vanilla extract
225 g plain flour
1 tsp baking powder
pinch of salt
10 small plums (or apricots)
icing sugar for dusting

Heat the oven to 180°C/Gas 4. Butter a 28 cm x 20 cm baking tin and line with greaseproof paper.

Cream the butter and sugar together until pale. Add the eggs, one at a time, beating well after each addition. Stir in the vanilla extract.

Sift the flour, baking powder and salt together over the mixture and fold in well, until combined. Spoon the mixture into the baking tin.

Cut the plums around their circumference, twist apart and remove the stone. Arrange the fruit, cut side up, in rows on top of the mixture. Bake for 30 minutes or until a thin skewer inserted in the cake comes out clean.

Cool slightly, or to room temperature. Dust with icing sugar, cut into squares and serve.

yoghurt

Yoghurt is the modern cook's cream; delicate, lush, delicious – and full of healthy germs. When these bacteria are added to milk, they break down the milk sugars, releasing lactic acid, which thickens the milk into yogurt and gives it a slightly sour taste. Choose thick low-fat, Greek-style yoghurt, or look for goat's and sheep's milk yoghurt in Greek shops and health food stores.

black pepper yoghurt Beat 1 tbsp icing sugar and 1 tbsp vodka into 400 g thick low-fat yoghurt. Scatter with roughly cracked black pepper and use as a dip for strawberries.

yoghurt cheese Place 500 g thick yoghurt in a large square of doubled muslin or cheesecloth and hang overnight to drain. Serve spoonfuls of yoghurt cheese drizzled with honey, or with ripe cherries.

mango raita Whisk 500 g thick yoghurt with 1 tbsp honey and 1 tbsp chopped mint. Mix with 1 diced mango, scatter with 1 tbsp desiccated coconut, and serve with cakes and puddings.

fruit fool Whiz 100 g raspberries and 1 tbsp icing sugar to a purée. Layer 200 g raspberries and 400 g thick yoghurt into 4 glasses, top with the berry purée, and serve with sponge fingers.

chocolate yoghurt Melt 100 g dark chocolate in a heatproof bowl set over a pan of gently simmering water, cool for 10 minutes and beat in 400 g low-fat yoghurt. Spoon over 8 pears or peaches, peeled and poached in sugar syrup.

caramel yoghurt Scatter 2 tbsp soft brown sugar over 300 g thick yoghurt and leave for 10 minutes to melt. Swirl the melted sugar through the yoghurt and serve with cakes, puds and poached fruits.

yoghurt ice-cream

Wow! Yoghurt is fantastic frozen, transformed into an incredibly refreshing 'ice-cream' that you can serve as a healthy dessert, scoop into ice-cream cones or sandwich between store-bought sesame snaps or wafers.

SERVES 4 TO 6

500 g thick Greek-style yoghurt
50 g icing sugar
OPTIONS
12 sesame snaps or wafer
   biscuits
2 tbsp good honey
50 g toasted walnuts or pecans

Whisk the yoghurt and icing sugar together, then churn in an ice-cream machine according to the manufacturer's instructions. Or, freeze in a loaf tin or plastic container for 1 hour, removing and beating the mixture three times at 30–minute intervals to break up the ice crystals, then freeze until firm. Soften for 15 to 30 minutes before serving.

Yoghurt ice-cream sandwiches: cut the ice-cream into blocks the same size as the sesame snaps, sandwich each block between two sesame snaps, then re-freeze on a tray until ready to serve.

Yoghurt ice-cream with honey and walnuts: cut into thick slabs, drizzle with honey, and scatter with toasted walnuts or pecans.

Soft-serve yoghurt ice-cream: remove from freezer after 2 to 3 hours when it is still all gloopy and soft. Serve in glasses with a drizzle of honey and scatter with toasted walnuts or pecans.

cranberry blondies

White chocolate makes elegantly pale blondies instead of the usual brunette brownies, and cranberries give them that little touch of pink that blondes love to wear. Cut into small cubes for coffee, or larger squares for those emergency chocolate situations.

MAKES 25 SMALL,
OR 9 LARGE

200 g butter, plus extra for tin
300 g quality white chocolate, chopped
3 medium eggs
150 g caster sugar
1/2 tsp pure vanilla extract
200 g plain flour, sifted
pinch of salt
1 tbsp grated orange zest
100 g dried cranberries
icing sugar for dusting

Heat the oven to 180°C/Gas 4. Lightly butter an 18 x 28 cm baking tin and line the base with greaseproof paper.

In a heatproof bowl set over a pan of barely simmering water, melt the butter with 150 g of the white chocolate, whisking well until smooth. Remove from the heat and allow to cool slightly.

In a separate bowl, beat the eggs, sugar and vanilla together until pale. Beat in the melted white chocolate mixture.

Fold in the flour and salt, then the remaining chopped chocolate, orange zest and 75 g of the cranberries. Pour into the baking tin and strew the rest of the cranberries on top. Bake for 20 minutes or until the top is firm and the inside is still a bit soft. Leave to cool in the tin.

Cut into small or large squares, dust with icing sugar and serve.

berry couscous

Couscous is the most elegant of comfort foods, especially when tossed with rose water and fresh berries that ping in the mouth. Serve with a sweet, creamy almond milk, for sipping, or for pouring over the top.

SERVES 4

300 g couscous
2 tbsp icing sugar
1 tsp rose water or orange
   blossom water
100 g blueberries
100 g raspberries
2 tbsp pistachios, sliced

ALMOND MILK

100 g ground almonds
$1/2$ tsp ground cinnamon
2 tbsp icing sugar
500 ml milk

To make the almond milk, combine the ground almonds, cinnamon, icing sugar and milk in a blender and whiz until smooth. Strain through a fine sieve, then pour into a bottle and chill.

Place the couscous and icing sugar in a large heatproof bowl. Pour 500 ml boiling water over the top, stir through, then cover and leave for 30 minutes until absorbed.

Break up the couscous and fluff it up a bit with your fingers. Add the rose water and berries and lightly toss.

Divide the couscous among four small bowls and scatter with pistachios. Shake the bottle of almond milk until frothy, and pour into four small chilled glasses to accompany the couscous.

sticky lemon pudding

This self-saucing pudding is a great family favourite, forming a pillow of soft golden lemon sponge cake on top, with a tangy lemony curd underneath.

SERVES 4

70 g butter, plus extra for
   the baking dish
180 g caster sugar
2 tsp grated lemon zest
3 medium eggs, separated
60 g plain flour, sifted
250 ml milk
100 ml lemon juice (around
   3 lemons)
icing sugar for dusting

Heat the oven to 180°C/Gas 4. In a food processor, beat the butter, sugar and lemon zest together until pale. Beat in the egg yolks, one at a time. Add the flour and milk alternately until you have a smooth batter, beating well. Lastly, beat in the lemon juice.

In a large bowl, beat the egg whites until firm but not stiff, and fold the two mixtures together.

Pour into a buttered 1 litre ovenproof dish and place in a baking tin. Half-fill the tin with hot water and bake for 50 minutes or until the pudding is lightly browned and set on top, with a soft base of gooey lemon curd.

Remove the dish from the water, dust the pudding with icing sugar and serve immediately.

good things to know

arborio rice A tough, plump superfino rice grown in Northern Italy. Use for risotto and rice puddings.

beancurd/tofu A bland white curd made from soya beans. Available fresh in soft (silken) and firm varieties, and in long-life packs.

black beans Salted, fermented black soy beans, available vacuum-packed or in cans from Chinese food stores. Throw a spoonful into stir-fries and noodle dishes.

buckwheat noodles/soba Dried buckwheat noodles available from Japanese specialists and health food stores. Great for cold noodle salads.

bulghur wheat Cracked wheat kernels available from Middle Eastern and health food stores.

capers The tiny green buds of a Mediterranean shrub. Buy in salt, and rinse before use. Available from good food stores and supermarkets.

cha plu A soft, tender green leaf (*piper sarmentosum*) used in Asian cooking. Sold in glossy, green bunches in Thai and Vietnamese food stores.

chicken stock To make your own, rinse 2 kg chicken bones and cover with 4 litres cold water. Bring to the boil, then simmer for 10 minutes, skimming off any froth. Add 2 finely sliced onions, 2 chopped carrots, 2 chopped celery stalks and 2 finely chopped leeks, and simmer for 2 to 3 hours, skimming occasionally. Strain, discarding bones and vegetables, and leave to cool. Refrigerate overnight. Remove any fat that has risen to the surface, and freeze until needed.

chinese rice wine Made from glutinous rice and used rather like sherry in cooking, Chinese rice wine, or *shao hsing*, is available from Asian food stores.

chocolate Choose the best quality dark chocolate with a high percentage of cocoa butter, eg 70%.

chorizo A Spanish pork sausage flavoured with paprika and garlic, sold dried and fresh.

couscous Tiny pearls of semolina used in both savoury and sweet dishes throughout the Middle East. Look for the pre-steamed 'instant' variety.

cranberries, dried American dried berries available from supermarkets and gourmet food stores.

daikon A large, long white radish, also known as mooli, with a refreshing flavour. Delicious freshly grated as a relish or slow-cooked in soups.

feta Salted fresh cheese sold in blocks at delicatessens, supermarkets and Greek food stores. Look for extra-creamy feta made from sheep's or goat's milk.

fish sauce A thin, salty sauce made from fermented fish and squid, used as a condiment in Thailand (nam pla) and Vietnam (nuoc mam).

harissa A spicy paste of dried red chillies and garlic. The best sort is available in jars from speciality food stores. If buying in tubes, dilute with olive oil and taste for strength before using.

hoisin sauce A thick, sweet pungent sauce made from fermented soy beans, sugar, vinegar, salt, garlic, chilli and sesame oil. A much nicer choice for pork or duck than the overly sweet plum sauce.

horseradish sauce A creamy, pungent condiment made from fiery horseradish, a root belonging to the crucifer family. Available from good food stores.

jalapeño chillies Keep a jar of pickled green jalapeños (pronounced *hal-a-pen-yos*) chillies in the fridge for those spontaneous taco moments. Available from major supermarkets.

jamon Fragrant cured ham, the Spanish equivalent of Italian prosciutto.

kaffir lime leaves Glossy leaves with a heavenly citrus smell. Fresh is best, available from Asian food stores.

mirin A light, sweet Japanese rice wine used for sauces, dressings and marinades. I love it in vinaigrettes as well. Available from Asian food stores and most supermarkets.

mozzarella Fresh mozzarella comes in smooth, milky white balls known as bocconcini, packed in their own whey. It is infinitely superior to mass-produced mozzarella. Delicate buffalo mozzarella, made from buffalo milk, is ruinously good.

olives Pay extra for good French, Greek, Spanish or Italian olives, and don't worry about stoning them. Avoid those awful pre-pitted, dyed-black olives that appear on cheap pizzas.

paprika My favourite is Spanish smoked paprika, with its rich smoky flavour and good heat levels.

pink peppercorns The small, dried red berries of the Brazilian pepper tree, with an aromatic peppery flavour. And yes, I only use them because they are pretty.

preserved lemons Whole lemons preserved in a salty brine, available from Middle Eastern specialists and major supermarkets. Rinse well, and use the rind only.

rice noodles Dried, flat, white, semi-transparent rice flour noodles, also known as rice stick noodles. Available in various widths.

rice vermicelli Dried, brittle semi-transparent noodles (thinner than rice noodles) made from extruded rice flour paste. These noodles turn white when cooked.

rice wine vinegar A clear, mild vinegar made from fermented rice, from Asian food stores. Fabulous with sliced cucumber and in salad dressings.

rose water A clear, light distillation of rose petals. Available from Middle Eastern stores and major supermarkets.

saffron The orange-red stigmas of the crocus plant. Expensive, but worth investing in and using sparingly. Crush with a tiny amount of water before adding to your cooking.

sea salt Upgrade to delicate sea salt flakes (eg Maldon) for table use. It makes all the difference in the world.

sesame oil A dark aromatic oil made from roasted sesame seeds, to be used sparingly in Asian food and in vinaigrettes.

shiitake mushrooms Dried black mushrooms that add rich, earthy flavour and a meaty texture to Asian dishes. To reconstitute, cover with boiling water and leave for at least 30 minutes before straining out any grit.

sugar Seek out natural unrefined sugars, for more flavour and health benefits.

tahini A thick, creamy, nutty paste made from husked and ground white sesame seeds. Available in jars from Middle Eastern specialists and health food stores.

tamarind concentrate A sour-tasting fruit sold as a pulp or, more conveniently, a refined concentrate in small jars available from supermarkets.

tobiko Very fine, crunchy Japanese fish roe, often coloured red, salmon orange or wasabi green. Available frozen from Japanese speciality stores.

togarashi A popular Japanese 'sprinkle' made of dried chilli, sansho pepper, sesame seeds and seaweed. Available from Japanese food stores.

tomato purée A concentrated tomato paste sold in small cartons, tubes, jars and cans.

tortillas Flat, unleavened pancakes made with corn or wheat flour. Available from supermarkets.

vanilla extract Pure vanilla extract is pricey, but so treacly and aromatic that you need use only a few drops. Avoid cheap vanilla essence, which is artificially flavoured.

vegetable stock I recommend Marigold Swiss Vegetable Bouillon Powder with its fresh, carroty taste. To make your own stock, heat 2 tbsp olive oil in a large pot. Add 2 finely sliced onions and 2 each finely chopped carrots, celery stalks and tomatoes. Cook for 5 minutes, stirring. Add 1.2 litres boiling water and simmer for 30 minutes. Strain, cool and freeze until needed.

wasabi A green pungent root, known as Japanese horseradish. Devilishly hot, available in a powder form (dilute with water to taste), or in tubes.

conversions

volume

5 ml	1 teaspoon (tsp)
10 ml	1 dessertspoon (dsp)
15 ml	1 tablespoon (tbsp)
20 ml	1 Australian tablespoon
30 ml	1 fl oz
40 ml	1$\frac{1}{2}$ fl oz
55 ml	2 fl oz
70 ml	2$\frac{1}{2}$ fl oz
85 ml	3 fl oz
90 ml	3$\frac{1}{2}$ fl oz
100 ml	3$\frac{3}{4}$ fl oz
115 ml	4 fl oz
125 ml	4$\frac{1}{2}$ fl oz
140 ml	5 fl oz
155 ml	5$\frac{1}{2}$ fl oz
170 ml	6 fl oz
185 ml	6$\frac{1}{2}$ fl oz
200 ml	7 fl oz
225 ml	8 fl oz
240 ml	8$\frac{1}{2}$ fl oz
255 ml	9 fl oz
285 ml	10 fl oz ($\frac{1}{2}$ pint)
350 ml	12 fl oz
375 ml	13 fl oz
400 ml	14 fl oz
425 ml	15 fl oz ($\frac{3}{4}$ pint)
450 ml	16 fl oz
565 ml	20 fl oz (1 pint)
710 ml	25 fl oz (1$\frac{1}{4}$ pints)
850 ml	30 fl oz (1$\frac{1}{2}$ pints)
1 litre	35 fl oz (1$\frac{3}{4}$ pints)
1.2 litres	2 pints

weight

7.5 g	$\frac{1}{4}$ oz
15 g	$\frac{1}{2}$ oz
20 g	$\frac{3}{4}$ oz
30 g	1 oz
40 g	1$\frac{1}{2}$ oz
55 g	2 oz
70 g	2$\frac{1}{2}$ oz
85 g	3 oz
90 g	3$\frac{1}{2}$ oz
115 g	4 oz
125 g	4$\frac{1}{2}$ oz
140 g	5 oz
170 g	6 oz
200 g	7 oz
225 g	8 oz
255 g	9 oz
285 g	10 oz
310 g	11 oz
340 g	12 oz
370 g	13 oz
400 g	14 oz
425 g	15 oz
455 g	1 lb
500 g	1 lb 2 oz
565 g	1 lb 4 oz
600 g	1 lb 5 oz
680 g	1 lb 8 oz
700 g	1 lb 9 oz
750 g	1 lb 10 oz
800 g	1 lb 12 oz
905 g	2 lb
1 kg	2 lb 3 oz

length

5 mm	$\frac{1}{4}$ inch
1 cm	$\frac{1}{2}$ inch
2.5 cm	1 inch
5 cm	2 inch
7.5 cm	3 inch
10 cm	4 inch
12 cm	5 inch
15 cm	6 inch
18 cm	7 inch
20 cm	8 inch
23 cm	9 inch
25 cm	10 inch
28 cm	11 inch
30 cm	12 inch

oven temperatures

140°C	275°F	Gas 1	Cool
150°C	300°F	Gas 2	Slow
170°C	325°F	Gas 3	Moderately slow
180°C	350°F	Gas 4	Moderate
190°C	375°F	Gas 5	Moderately hot
200°C	400°F	Gas 6	Hot
220°C	425°F	Gas 7	Hot
230°C	450°F	Gas 8	Very hot

index

acknowledgements

The publishers wish to thank the following companies for the loan of props for photography:

Designers Guild, King's Road, London SW3;

Divertimenti, 33/4 Marylebone High Street, London W1;

Skandium, 86 Marylebone High Street, London W1.